Enjoy English with Charlie Brown and Friends

【Revised Edition】

Haruko Toyama

Language and Culture in *Peanuts*

NAN'UN-DO

Preface

1. Why *Peanuts*?

I am a lifelong fan of *Peanuts*, not only because of its terrific characters, great good humor, and sharp insights into modern life and culture, but also because of its wonderful language. Nothing in fact could be simpler, more natural, more effective—more beautiful. Let's face it: *Peanuts* is an icon. Its enduring influence on our life and times is undeniable. A classic example is Linus's "security blanket," an ingenious phrase and concept that soon found its way into every standard English dictionary and quickly became a metaphor for a universal human longing.

Peanuts abounds with such vital contributions to our language and culture. So I thought: Shouldn't everyone have the opportunity to read and appreciate at least a few of these immortal comic strips? And then I thought: Why not find a way to use *Peanuts* to help students gain a good, solid grasp of practical, everyday English and, at the same time, encourage them to explore a wide variety of cultural as well as moral and philosophical issues? This textbook is the result.

2. How It Works

Each lesson is divided into two parts, each of which is introduced by a *Peanuts* strip. The first half of the lesson uses words and expressions found in the first strip to focus in on practical language instruction—vocabulary acquisition, proper usage, listening comprehension, basic composition, and so on. The second half deals with the weightier themes hinted at in the second strip: personal and group identity, disappointment and hope, gender stereotypes, social order and nonconformity, to name just a few.

3. Who It's For

Although I wrote this textbook with college students in mind, I am confident that anyone looking for a fresh, fun approach to practical English learning will find it useful and stimulating. There is much to enjoy here—first and foremost, of course, the *Peanuts* strips themselves. I invite even those with certain attitudes towards English learning—perhaps crabs like Lucy or timid souls like Charlie Brown—to give this textbook a try. I think you'll be pleasantly surprised.

4. Thanks

First of all, I am indebted to Charles Schulz. No matter how many times I read your comics, they fill me with warmth and smiles. Happiness is being with the "gang" you've created. I am also very grateful to Yoshihito Katagiri, who, once again, kindly contributed his consummate editing skills and conscientiousness to this work. I could not have done it without you. To the superb editorial team of Nan'un-do, especially Atsushi Kato and Jim Knudsen, thank you so much for giving me this opportunity. William Lindsey at the University of Kansas patiently read my manuscript and offered valuable suggestions. I could not have written the cultural essays if I had not met my teacher and mentor Thomas Gregor at Vanderbilt many years ago. Lastly, my deep appreciation goes out to my students who have given me critical and supportive feedback. Nothing has been more joyful for me than sharing the wonderful world of *Peanuts* with you.

Haruko Toyama

はじめに

1. なぜピーナッツなのでしょうか？

私は生涯ピーナッツファンの一人です。素晴らしい登場人物たち、洗練されたユーモア、現代文化や生活への鋭い洞察力だけでなく、漫画の中の言葉にも魅了されます。実際、ピーナッツの漫画の台詞のようにシンプルで、自然で、効果的で、そして美しい言葉は他にないかもしれません。正直なところ、ピーナッツはすでに文化的アイコンと言えましょう。この漫画が長きにわたり人々の人生や時代に与え続けてきた影響には疑問の余地がありません。例えばその代表的なものの１つに、登場人物の一人、ライナスが抱えているセキュリティーブランケット（安心毛布）があります。この言葉は、このピーナッツの漫画をきっかけとして現在ではほとんどのスタンダードな英語の辞書に載るようになり、さらには〝自分にとって大事で不可欠なもの〟という比喩的な意味を持つ言葉となって世界に広まっていきました。

ピーナッツの世界が私たちの言語や文化へ与えてくれる恩恵には計り知れないものがあります。そこでこう考えてみました。この不朽のコミックを誰もが読んで楽しみ味わう機会をもっと持てたらよいのではないか。そしてこうも考えました。実用的な、日常で使われる英語をしっかり理解するための手段として、また同時に、世界の多種多様な文化的事柄、さらにはあえて言ってしまいますが、倫理的で哲学的な事柄にも思考をめぐらせてゆく手段として、学生向けにピーナッツを使える方法を探してみたらどうだろう、と。その気持ちからこの本が生まれました。

2. どのようにして？

各章のレッスンは２つの部分から成り、それぞれの部分は２つの異なるピーナッツの漫画で始まっています。各レッスンの前半は、１つめの漫画の中に含まれている語彙や表現に基づいた実践的な英語の練習に焦点を当てています。具体的には、語彙の習得、表現用法の習得、リスニングの理解、そして基本的な英作文などの問題を揃えました。そして後半は、２つめの漫画からヒントを得た少しシリアスなテーマのリーディングが扱われています。少し例を挙げてみますと、個人やグループのアイデンティティ、失望と希望、ジェンダーのステレオタイプ、社会の秩序と文化の多様性などといったようなテーマです。

3. どなたに向けて？

大学生の使用を心においてこのテキストを書きましたが、実用的な英語を、フレッシュで、楽しいアプローチで学習したいと探しておられる方ならどなたでも、きっと役に立ち面白いと感じていただけることを願っています。楽しめる内容が沢山つまっていますが、まず何と言っても、ピーナッツの漫画そのものがとにかく楽しめるのです。それから英語の学習に対して、ある種の態度を持っている学生…ルーシーのようにすぐ文句を言いたがる学生、あるいはチャーリー・ブラウンのように今ひとつ自信のない学生も…ぜひこのテキストを試してみて下さい。きっと嬉しい驚きがあるかもしれませんよ。

4. 感謝をこめて

チャールズ・シュルツさん、どんな時も貴方のコミックを読めば、いつも温かさと微笑みで心が満たされます。幸せはピーナッツのメンバーと一緒にいること。この度改訂版を出版するにあたり再度ご参加くださった編集者の片桐嘉人さん、綿密な編集技術と根気の要る大変な作業への取り組み、ご協力に深く感謝しております。南雲堂編集部の方々、特に加藤敦編集長と優れた英語教育者のジム・クヌーセン先生に心より御礼申し上げます。カンザス大学のウイリアム・リンゼイさん、原稿を辛抱強く読み貴重なアドバイスを下さいました。尊敬するトーマス・グレゴー先生、何年も前にヴァンダビルト大学でお会いしていなかったら、このテキストのエッセイは創れなかったことでしょう。

最後になりましたが、キャラクターを愛し、貴重なフィードバックをくださる学生の皆さん、私にとって皆さんとピーナッツの世界を分かち合えるほど嬉しいことはないんです。ありがとうございました。

外山晴子

To the Students

Welcome to the wonderful world of Charlie Brown and friends. I have written this textbook based on classic *Peanuts* comic strips with two main goals in mind: (1) to help you improve your everyday English reading, listening, writing, and speaking skills; and (2) to introduce you to some of the more important cross-cultural topics and social issues suggested by the strips themselves. *Peanuts* has given me countless hours of pleasure and taught me more than I can say. I'm sure the cartoons in this textbook will do the same for you.

How to Use This Book

Each of the text's thirteen lessons features two *Peanuts* comic strips. These are followed by several skill-building exercises that I believe are as fun as they are effective (to be really effective, learning should be fun). The following is an explanation of the basic format of the lessons, with suggestions for how you can get as much out of them as possible. (The Audio mark in the text indicates a listening exercise that uses the audio-files (mp3) at nanun-do.com.)

Cartoon 1—— This first cartoon is used mainly as a basis for practical language study and practice. The exercises that follow the cartoon are built up around words and expressions that appear in it. Charlie Brown cartoons aren't always as simple as they seem, so make sure you take your time reading them.

Setting the Scene—— This is a brief explanation of **Cartoon 1** that will help you understand it better and enjoy it more. Remember: the "plot," theme, and humor of a *Peanuts* comic strip are often quite subtle.

Guess the Words—— This is a quick spelling and vocabulary quiz. All you have to do is complete the spelling of a few words that are related in meaning or subject matter to a key word in **Cartoon 1**.

Everyday Expressions—— This exercise takes three common words from **Cartoon 1** and uses them in sample sentences. Just read the sentences, repeat them after your teacher, and memorize them.

Mini-Application—— This exercise asks you to try your hand at translating one or two short Japanese sentences into English using the words and expressions you have learned in the lesson so far. You may find this kind of full-sentence writing a little challenging at first, but you'll soon surprise yourself at how good you are at it.

Verb Review—— This is the last activity based on **Cartoon 1**. It has three parts. This first part takes a basic verb from the cartoon—make, give, come, etc.—and explains how it is used in a variety of common colloquial or idiomatic phrases.

Listen and Repeat —— In this second part of the **Verb Review** section, the basic verb is used in several short sentences. Read the sentences and make sure you know what they mean (some are a little "tricky"). If you're not sure, get a little help from your teacher. Then repeat them after the Audio or your teacher.

Listen and Write —— In this final part of **Verb Review**, the basic verb appears in two or three short dialogues with some words missing in each. As you listen to the dialogues, fill in the blanks. When you've finished, practice the dialogues with a partner.

Cartoon 2—— This second cartoon is usually a little more challenging than the first, so read it carefully. If you're not sure what its "point" is, don't worry: the reading that follows should clear it up for you.

Reading —— This is a 300-400-word essay dealing with the cultural, social, and even philosophical themes suggested by **Cartoon 2**. Because of their subject matter, the essays may initially be somewhat difficult for you to fully grasp, but with a little extra effort, I'm sure you'll soon get used to them and, I believe, get a lot out of them. And by the way, if you're hoping to boost your TOEIC and/or TOEFL reading scores, the essays will help you increase your vocabulary and give you plenty of good reading-comprehension practice.

Comprehension—— The four simple multiple-choice questions that make up this exercise check your understanding of the essay's most important details and ideas.

Think It Over—— This final activity consists of two thought-provoking questions. It gives you a chance to think about and discuss the lesson's main ideas. It consists of two questions. Read the questions, think them over, perhaps write out a short answer, and, if time permits, discuss them with a partner or in a small group.

Coffee Break—— The four Coffee Break sections (which appear after lessons 3, 6, 9 and 12) are just that—a little break from the regular lessons. They are made up of two parts. The first part asks you to read and enjoy a longer, Sunday-edition strip that deals with a popular running gag in *Peanuts*: Lucy's using a variety of tricks to get Charlie Brown to try to kick a football, again and again, only to fail each time. The second part is a Search and Circle puzzle that is just for fun — though it takes some skill, too.

学生の皆さんへ

チャーリー・ブラウンと仲間たちの素晴らしい世界にようこそ！ このテキストはピーナッツの漫画を基に、主に 2 つの目標を念頭において作られています。まず 1）リーディング、リスニング、ライティング、そしてスピーキングの総合的な英語運用能力を伸ばすこと、そして 2）漫画から示唆される比較文化的なトピックや問題に親しむことです。ピーナッツは私に沢山の喜びをもたらしてくれただけでなく、多くのことを教えてくれました。このテキストも皆さんにとってそうなればいいなと願っています。

本書の構成と使用法

13 章から成るテキストの各レッスンは、2 つのピーナッツの漫画から構成され、漫画の後にスキルを身につけるためのいくつかのエクササイズが続いています。エクササイズは実用的でかつ楽しいものです。効果をあげるためにも楽しく学習しましょう。

このテキストをより良く活用するためのレッスンの基本的な構成を、以下に説明してあります。ヘッドホンのマークはテキスト付属の音声を使用するリスニングのエクササイズです。

Cartoon 1—— 1 つめの漫画は実践的な語学力を伸ばすためのものです。この漫画の後に、語彙や表現に関連したいくつかのエクササイズが用意されています。チャーリー・ブラウンの漫画は一見すると簡単そうに見えますが、実は中々奥深いものです。時間をかけて解釈しましょう。

Setting the Scene—— 1 つめの漫画の短い説明です。ピーナッツの話の筋、テーマ、ユーモアは、ほとんどの場合、ドラマティックなものでなくむしろ非常に示唆的で subtle な（さりげない）ものだと覚えておいて下さい。

Guess the Words—— 語彙のスペリングクイズです。漫画の中に入っているキーワードと意味的または内容的に関係するいくつかの単語の綴りを、完成してみましょう。

Everyday Expressions—— 漫画の中の語彙または表現の使い方が、3 つの例文で示されています。例文を読み先生の後について発音し、できればセンテンスごと覚えてしまいましょう。

Mini-Application—— ここまでのエクササイズで学んだ語彙や表現を応用して、1 つか 2 つの日本文を英語に訳してみましょう。文章を丸ごと作ってみるのは、最初は少し大変かもしれませんが、すぐにコツがわかり上手になるでしょう。

Verb Review―― 1 つめの漫画に関連した最後のエクササイズです。まず make, give, come などの基本動詞が毎回 1 つ取り上げられ、そのニュアンスや口語的なフレーズが紹介されています。

Listen and Repeat ―― 1 つめの漫画の中に登場する基本動詞がいくつかの短い文章で使われています。文章を読み意味を確認しましょう。そして付属音声または先生の後についてリピートしてみて下さい。

Listen and Write ―― 今度は空欄のある短い会話の中で、上記の基本動詞が使われています。会話を聞きとりながら空欄を埋めて文を完成してみましょう。（中には少し“ひっかかりそうな”ものも入っていますよ！）時間があればペアでも会話を練習してみて下さい。

Cartoon 2―― 2 つめの漫画です。最初の漫画よりも少しチャレンジングなものが多いかもしれませんが、じっくり解釈してみて下さい。後に続くリーディングでも漫画の主旨が確認できるでしょう。

Reading ―― 2 つめの漫画が示唆するテーマをヒントとした 300 ～ 400 字程度の社会文化的なリーディングです。レッスンによってはややフィロソフィカルなものも含まれています。トピックによっては初めはやや難しく感じるかもしれませんが、すぐに慣れて楽しめるようになるでしょう。ところでこのセクションは、TOEIC や TOEFL のリーディングセクションのスコアを向上させたい人にとっても、語彙を増やし読解力をつける練習として役立つでしょう。

Comprehension―― リーディングの理解を確認するための 4 つの選択式の問題です。

Think It Over―― 最後のアクティヴィティーはリーディングと関連する 2 つの質問から成っています。質問を読み、よく考えてみましょう。実際に自分の答えを書いてみたり、あるいはペアやグループでディスカッションしてみてもよいでしょう。

Coffee Break―― テキストの 4 カ所にあるコーヒーブレイクのセクション（レッスン 3、6、9、12 の後）は通常のレッスンの息抜きのようなつもりで楽しんで下さい。コーヒーブレイクは 2 つの部分から成ります。まずピーナッツの中でも定番のジョークの 1 つを、通常より長めの日曜版の漫画で読んでみましょう。アメリカの歴代大統領にも人気のあったこのフットボールシリーズの漫画では、毎回チャーリー・ブラウンにフットボールを蹴らせようとしてルーシーがトリックを仕掛けます。チャーリー・ブラウンはいつもあの手この手で騙されて失敗してしまうのです。もう 1 つは言葉探しパズルです。楽しんでトライしてみて下さい。

Contents

目次

Characters in *Peanuts*

Peanuts has a large cast of fascinating characters, but in this text, we will spend most of our time with the ten lovable characters below.

Lucy Van Pelt

Always loud and critical. In her advice booth she becomes a "doctor." Loves Schroeder. Right fielder on the baseball team.

ルーシー

得意なのは人の批判。時々精神分析スタンドを“開業”する。シュローダーに一方的に恋の攻撃をする。野球ではライト。

Charlie Brown

Snoopy's tenderhearted owner. Sincere, shy, and lonely. Longs for the little red-haired girl. Pitcher and manager of a terrible baseball team. Based loosely on his creator, Charles Schulz.

チャーリー・ブラウン

心優しいスヌーピーの飼い主。誠実で内気で淋しがり屋。赤毛の女の子に憧れている。連戦連敗の野球チームでは監督兼ピッチャー。何をしても失敗ばかりだがロマンティスト。作者チャールズ・シュルツと重なる部分が多い。

Linus Van Pelt

Lucy's brother. Gentle and philosophical. Rarely without his famous security blanket. Firmly believes in the Great Pumpkin.

ライナス

ルーシーの弟。人生を深く見つめる哲学者。安心毛布を抱えハロウィンのカボチャ大王の到来を信じている。

Peppermint Patty

The best athlete among the *Peanuts* gang. Manager of her own baseball team. Calls Charlie Brown "Chuck."

ペパーミント パティ

ピーナッツの中で一番スポーツが得意な女の子。自分の野球チームの監督。チャーリー・ブラウンをチャックと呼んでいる。

Pigpen

Attracts dust wherever he goes. Charlie Brown is one of the few people who understand him. He plays third base.

ピッグペン

どこへ行くにも埃を惹きつけてしまう。彼の個性はチャーリー・ブラウンには理解されている。野球では三塁手。

Woodstock
Snoopy's close friend. Instead of "migrating," he often stays at Snoopy's doghouse.

ウッドストック
スヌーピーの親友。渡り鳥だが、渡らずに、スヌーピーの住まいの回りで暮らしていることが多い。

Sally
Sister of Charlie Brown. Hates school, study, and hard work. Loves Linus.

サリー
チャーリー・ブラウンの妹。学校と勉強が大嫌い。ライナスのことが好き。

Snoopy
A beagle who thinks and acts like a human. Imagines he is a Flying Ace (WWI pilot), novelist, lawyer, and many other successful people.

スヌーピー
自分のことをイヌと思っていないビーグル犬。飛行士、小説家、弁護士などいろいろな人物に変身する。

Schroeder
Plays a toy piano. Loves Beethoven. Catcher on the baseball team.

シュローダー
クラシックピアノが趣味。ベートーヴェンを心から尊敬している。
野球ではキャッチャー。

Rerun Van Pelt
Baby brother of Lucy and Linus. Likes to play with Snoopy.

リラン
ルーシーとライナスの弟。時々スヌーピーと遊びたがる。

LESSON 1

Menu

- Make sure you can ...
- Body Language in *Peanuts*

Cartoon 1

Read and enjoy this comic strip.

Setting the Scene

For Snoopy, the secret of a successful life is to always be positive about the future, but, at the same time, to be very cautious. But what's most important in life for him is ...

スヌーピーによれば、成功する人生の秘訣は、まず将来に対して前向きであること、同時に慎重であること。でもそれにもまして大事なのは…

Guess the Words

Complete these words that are related to "supper."

d__nn__r	br__nch	des__ert
app__tizer	re__ta__rant	Today's Sp__cial

Everyday Expressions

Read and memorize these expressions and sentences.

❶ the secret of ...

What is *the secret of* your success?

❷ look ahead

You should *look ahead* to your future career.

❸ look back

She walked straight ahead without *looking back*.

Mini-Application

Translate this sentence into English using the words and expressions above.

成功の秘訣ですって？　いつも前向きに、同時に慎重であるようにしています。

Verb Review

Make sure you can still see ...
…があるのをしっかり確かめて

人生の秘訣の中でも、晩ご飯があるのをちゃんと確かめるのこそ大事なこと！とは現実的なスヌーピーらしい考えですね。make sure は“確かめる”という意味です。make は“作り出す”が基本ですが、作られるものは make a cake（ケーキを作る）make some money（お金を稼ぐ）make a plan（計画を立てる）などさまざまです。make a difference（違いを出す、意義深くする）make a point（一理ある）など口語的なフレーズも覚えましょう。また What makes you say so?（なぜそう思うの？）のように“させる”という意味も表現できます。

Listen and Repeat

02

Repeat these sentences after the audio.

1. You've made my day!
2. Make yourself at home.
3. I'm afraid I won't be able to make it to the party.
4. Sorry, but I made a mistake.
5. He made the final decision.
6. May I make a small suggestion?

Listen and Write

03

Listen and fill in the blanks in these short dialogues.

1. W: You (　　　　　) your (　　　　　) again!
   M: Sorry. How can I make it up to you?

2. W: Professor Smith, may I take a make-up test?
   M: All right. I'll make it a take-home test. But you've got to (　　　　　) it in on (　　　　　).

3. W: How are you making out with your (　　　　　) (　　　　　)?
   M: Well, I'm still sending out resumés.

4. W: I don't have a (　　　　　)! This is the (　　　　　) of the world for me!
   M: Why do you always make such a big deal out of everything?

Cartoon 2

Read and enjoy this comic strip.

❶

* can't stand　耐えられないよ
* go through　体験する
* completely = totally
* bill　請求書

❷

❸

❹
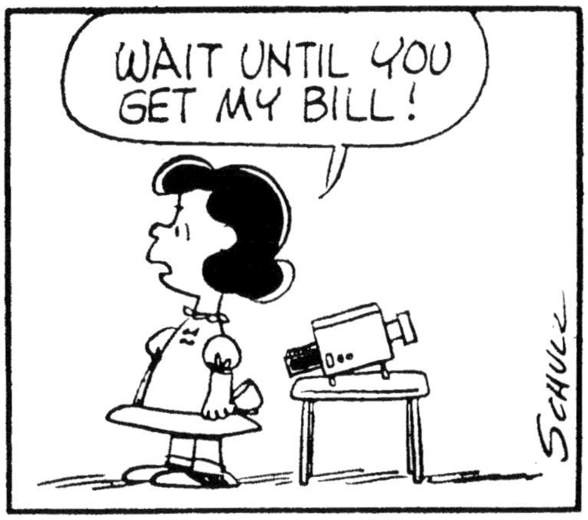

自分の欠点（faults）の数々を映像で見せられたチャーリー・ブラウン。悩み相談に応じる“精神分析医”ルーシーとしては、これもセラピーの仕事のうち。でも彼はショックで叫びだしちゃいます。

Reading

04

Body Language in *Peanuts*

赤毛の女の子には気持ちを打ち明けられず、友達に理解されない時はがっくりとうなだれてしまうチャーリー・ブラウン。でも感情を表せるのは言葉だけではないはず。今回はボディランゲージについてのエッセイを読んでみましょう。

Charlie Brown is the shiest, most reflective, and most considerate of all the characters in *Peanuts*. He is not very good at expressing his feelings, especially when Lucy is yelling at him. Other kids often tease him because he fails at almost everything he tries. Just as Charles Schulz, *Peanuts*' creator, yearned for a certain girl when he was a young man, Charlie Brown yearns to talk to "the little red-haired girl" who goes to his school. But Charlie Brown is always too shy to strike up a conversation with her. When he feels lonely and depressed, he walks to Lucy's psychiatry stand with his head down and his hands in his pockets, and a nickel ready to give her. Just by looking closely at Charlie Brown — the expression on his face, how he holds his arms — we can pick up on his feelings even without reading the dialogue. This type of "non-verbal communication" is called body language.

Our body language conveys messages without words through facial expressions, eye contact, touch, posture, and gestures. Are we slouching or standing tall? Shall we hug or shake hands? Lock eyes or look down? Like verbal language, body language varies across cultures. Eye contact, for example, is valued in Euro-American interaction, but in many Asian contexts, direct eye contact is often considered rude or even intimidating. The "OK" gesture (thumb and index finger shaped into an "O," with the other fingers out straight) is another good example. It can mean "all right" in the U.S., is a sexual insult in Brazil, and often refers to money in Japan. Another body language is the thumbs-up gesture, which means "OK" or "excellent" in the U.S., but is considered offensive throughout the Arab world.

Some forms of body language such as facial expressions may not be learned behavior at all, but instead demonstrate the universality of human emotions. Laughing and smiling may be one such universal expression. When one person starts to laugh, those around that person can't help but feel good and start laughing, too. As the old saying goes, "Laugh and the world laughs with you." Perhaps Charlie Brown should try laughing more. This might make him feel better and save himself both a nickel and a trip to Lucy's stand.

NOTES 5. yearn 憧れる、恋しく思う　5. "the little red-haired girl" チャーリー・ブラウンが憧れている赤毛の女の子。漫画ではその姿は出てこない。　6. strike up ~ ～はじめる　7. Lucy' s psychiatry stand ルーシーが皆の悩み相談に応じる精神分析スタンド　7. a nickel = 5 cents　9. pick up on 気づく　12. hug 抱擁する　16. index finger 人差し指

Comprehension

Circle the best choice.

1. Charlie Brown's personality can be described as _________.
   a. moody
   b. introverted
   c. outgoing

2. Body language includes _________.
   a. facial expressions only
   b. gestures only
   c. gestures, touching, and facial expressions

3. What do Americans show with a thumbs-up sign?
   a. excellence
   b. offensiveness
   c. indifference

4. Which sentence best summarizes the main idea of the essay?
   a. Body language is more important than verbal language.
   b. The meaning of body language changes over time.
   c. Body language varies from culture to culture, but it is also universal.

Think It Over

Q. What body language in others makes you feel comfortable or uncomfortable?

Q. What gestures in Japanese culture are considered rude or taboo?

LESSON 2

Menu

- I feel like giving you a hug ...
- Lucy's Psychiatry Stand

Cartoon 1

Read and enjoy this comic strip.

Setting the Scene

Lucy's feelings toward Snoopy are ambivalent. He irritates her at times, but at other times, he is so lovable that she can't help wanting to hug him. Snoopy takes her and others' comments with an air of self-confidence. "How attractive I am!" he likes to think.

ルーシーのスヌーピーへの気持ちは少し複雑です。スヌーピーなんて気にいらない！と感じる時も。だけどやっぱり可愛いので時には抱きしめたくなっちゃう。一方、人間にどんなことを言われてもスヌーピーは楽天的で自信ありげです。やっぱりボクって魅力的なんだなあ。

Guess the Words

Complete these words that are related to "admit."

ac__ept　　ack__owle__ge　　r__cog__ize

re__lize　　ag__ee

Everyday Expressions

Read and memorize these expressions and sentences.

❶ there are times when ...

There are times when I feel that I can do anything.

❷ but I must admit ...

I don't like him that much, *but I must admit* he is very talented.

❸ feel like ...

I'm bored. I *feel like* going out today.

Mini-Application

Translate this sentence into English using the words and expressions above.

学校に行く気がしない時がある。でも友達にはやっぱり会いたいと思う。
（＝会いたいということを自分は認めなくてはいけない）

Verb Review

I feel like **giving** you a hug ...

抱きしめたい気分…

たいていイジワル気分なルーシーですが、本当はスヌーピーの良い友達です。give you a hug は“抱きしめる”という意味ですが、同じような使い方で give you a call（電話する）give you a notice（通知する）などの表現があります。贈り物など具体的なものからアイデアや励ましのような抽象的なものまで“与える”のが give の基本イメージです。give up（あきらめる）give away（無償で与える、ゆずる）などいろいろなイディオムの形でもよく使われます。

Listen and Repeat

Repeat these sentences after the audio.

05

1. Give me a break.
2. She gave me some good advice.
3. Don't give up so easily.
4. Give, and expect nothing in return.
5. I'm willing to give it a shot.
6. (at a restaurant) Would you give me the check, please?

Listen and Write

Listen and fill in the blanks in these short dialogues.

06

1. W: Your (　　　　　) was very well written.
   M: Thanks. I gave it a (　　　　　) of thought.
2. W: I have an (　　　　　) tomorrow.
   M: Good luck. I'm sure you'll give a very good (　　　　　).
3. M: Would you give me a call when you get (　　　　　)?
   W: I will, but it might be pretty (　　　　　).
4. W: Professor Smith, who is your (　　　　　) composer?
   M: Give me Mozart any (　　　　　).

Cartoon 2

Read and enjoy this comic strip.

❶

＊ sort of　何て言うか…
＊ for quite some time　かなり長い間
＊ get better　気分が良くなる

❷

❸

❹

これまで長いこと精神分析スタンドに通っているのに、ちっとも効果がないみたい…と不平(complaint)をもらすチャーリー・ブラウン。でもそんな苦情にもどこ吹く風のルーシーは？

Reading

07

Lucy's Psychiatry Stand

時々精神分析スタンドを開業し、みんなの悩み相談に応じるルーシー。仲間の子供相手ですが、料金もしっかり取りたてます。ルーシーにかぎらず私たちは得ることがリッチになることと思いがちなのですが、社会によっては…

Every now and then Lucy opens her psychiatry stand and becomes a doctor for the neighborhood kids. She accepts any client or patient as long as he or she has a nickel, but her main client is Charlie Brown. Although Lucy believes that she is a very competent doctor, her advice hardly ever does Charlie Brown any real good. He remains pessimistic, shy, and even a little lonely. Lucy's consulting fee is 5 cents for an "opinion," 10 cents for her "thoughts for the day," and 25 cents for "sound advice." Of course, Lucy is just a kid and not a real psychiatrist. But stands like Lucy's doctor's stand are a very real American phenomenon.

American kids often put up stands—usually just a table with a sign on it—in front of their houses in summertime. These stands mostly sell cold drinks like homemade lemonade to passersby. Some sell home-grown fruits and vegetables. The children decide the prices themselves. Setting prices and selling goods on their own allows these kids to experience a "money economy." Many American children also receive an allowance in return for doing various chores around the house, like washing the dishes, taking out the garbage, and running errands for their parents.

In societies like America and Japan, success often means "gaining more" through making money. Like Lucy, most of us would like to make money and become rich. In some other cultures, however, giving things away is regarded as the best way to become "rich." One example is the potlatch. This was a traditional gift-giving ceremony performed by groups of Native Americans in the Pacific Northwest of the United States and in Canada's British Columbia. Potlatch means "providing food" or "consumption." People hosted feasts at which they gave away most of their wealth and material goods. In such societies, people who give away their wealth are considered to be truly rich. They gain everyone's respect—and gain in social status, as well.

It is hard to imagine Lucy giving away all of her nickels, dimes, and quarters. It is easy to imagine, however, how much Charlie Brown, Linus, Schroeder, and the rest of the gang would admire her if she did.

NOTES 3. competent 有能な 10. passersby 通行人 12. allowance お小遣い 24. dimes: one dime = 10 cents 24. quarters: one quarter = 25 cents 25. the gang ピーナッツに登場する子供たち

Comprehension

Circle the best choice.

1. Lucy consults with __________.

   a. Charlie Brown only

   b. rich kids only

   c. any kid who can pay

2. What is the main reason that some American kids sell lemonade in summertime?

   a. They like making cold drinks.

   b. They want to make money.

   c. They want to help people stay cool on hot days.

3. What do some Native Americans gain by holding a potlatch?

   a. land

   b. wealth

   c. social status

4. Which sentence best summarizes the main idea of the essay?

   a. Children need to understand the value of money.

   b. The meaning of "rich" varies depending on what a particular society values most.

   c. Lucy is a good doctor because she only charges a nickel for each opinion she gives.

Think It Over

Q. Did you receive an allowance when you were a child? If so, what did you do to earn it? If not, why not?

Q. Have you ever volunteered your time or donated money to a cause you think is important? What was the cause? How did volunteering make you feel?

LESSON 3

Menu

- I can't run my office ...
- Friends Forever

Cartoon 1

Read and enjoy this comic strip.

Setting the Scene

Lucy gets mad at Snoopy because she hasn't received payment for the counseling she gave him. Business is business. She lets Snoopy know—sarcastically—that she's not in psychiatry for her own mental health. She's in it for the money.

スヌーピーの悩み相談にのって治療してあげたのに、支払いを受けていないルーシーは怒り心頭。ビジネスはビジネス。きっちり払ってもらわなくちゃ。だって、精神分析医は自分たちの精神を気持ちよくするためにやっているんじゃなくて、利益のためにやっているのよっ。

Guess the Words

Complete these words that are related to "business."

co__pa__y　　fi__m　　ent__rpri__e　　c__mme__ce

m__nag__ment　　n__goti__tions　　entre__reneur

Everyday Expressions

Read and memorize these expressions and sentences.

❶ cure

Prevention is better than *cure*.

❷ business

She is very successful in *business*.

It's my decision. Please mind your own *business*.

Mini-Application

Translate this sentence into English using the words and expressions above.

ビジネスをする上で一番大事なのは何だと思いますか？
交渉能力と言っていいでしょうね。　　（能力 = skill）

Verb Review

I can't **run** my office ...

オフィスを経営していけないのよっ…

心の治療をしてあげたのに相談料がまだなので、スヌーピーに怒っているルーシー。そう、彼女のビジネスも“顧客”の支払いがあってこそです。office は会社や事務所だけでなく、大学での研究室、あるいはルーシーの精神分析スタンドのようなちょっとした仕事場を指すこともあります。“スピーディーにある方向に走る、動く”というのが動詞 run のイメージですが、学校や会社などを運営・経営する、選挙などに立候補するという意味もあります。今回は run のいろいろな表現を学びましょう。

Listen and Repeat

08

Repeat these sentences after the audio.

1. Mary wants to run away from home.
2. He is running for class president.
3. My mom runs a small business.
4. I ran into an old classmate yesterday.
5. My contract runs out next month.
6. I hate to run, but I have a dentist appointment.

Listen and Write

09

Listen and fill in the blanks in these short dialogues.

1. W: A lot of my (   ) are musicians.
   M: How cool! Musical (   ) seems to run in your family.

2. W: Gosh, this multi-function (   ) is really expensive.
   M: It is, but in the long run, it will (   ) you money.

3. W: We are about to run (   ) (   ) gas.
   M: We'd better pull in at the (   ) gas station and fill up.

4. W: What do people study in an MBA (   )?
   M: Well, such things as how to run a (   ) business, for example.

Cartoon 2

Read and enjoy this comic strip.

* Here we are ...　これっていいよね…
* sharing　わけ合う
* I can tell you ~　ほんとに～だと思うよ。

スヌーピーと一緒にピクニック。チャーリー・ブラウンはなんて幸せそうな様子でしょう。でも現実的なスヌーピーは…

Reading

10

Friends Forever

自由な思考で自分の世界を作り出すスヌーピーと、心配や悩みがいつも頭から離れないチャーリー・ブラウン。彼らの関係は典型的なペットとその飼い主とはちょっと違います。むしろ彼らは現代に生きる私たちの姿そのものと言えるかもしれません。

At first glance, Charlie Brown's relationship with Snoopy might seem to be a stereotypical one of owner and faithful dog. Charlie Brown often imagines their relationship as being that of two very close friends, with each feeling love and respect for the other. Snoopy, however, has different ideas about it. Although he likes Charlie Brown, he has no concept of being useful or faithful to his owner. In fact, he does not even see Charlie Brown as his owner—or himself as a dog. While Charlie Brown lives for Snoopy, Snoopy lives for himself.

These two contrasting personalities represent more than the relationship between a boy and his dog. Charlie Brown and Snoopy also represent two different approaches to living. Charlie Brown struggles to cope with everyday life while Snoopy lives as a free spirit.

Charlie Brown feels that he does not fit in well in the world and, at times, seems overwhelmed by it. He feels isolated from everyone, and yet he yearns to be loved by everyone, too. This isolation intensifies on holidays in particular, because he never receives a Christmas or Valentine's Day card from anyone. He often goes to Lucy's psychiatry stand to talk to her about all of his anxieties. But he is unable simply to say "Hi" to the little red-haired girl he so badly wants to talk to. Despite his love of baseball, as a pitcher he can never manage to win a game for his neighborhood team. The challenges and competitiveness of life often leave Charlie Brown feeling left behind, alone, and disappointed.

Snoopy, however, has a completely different approach to life. Instead of struggling to fit in in the world, Snoopy creates his own world using his unrestricted imagination. In this imaginary world, he can become a novelist, a flying ace, a professional tennis player, a lawyer—anything that strikes his fancy. Rather than being overwhelmed by the world, Snoopy ignores it and lives as he wishes.

We feel empathy toward Charlie Brown because we know that we, too, have to struggle to find our place in this world. As for Snoopy, well, we envy him. He embodies our desire to live our lives on our own terms. As boy and beagle, Charlie Brown and Snoopy are friends, but they also stand for two contrasting ways of thinking about life: life as it really is, and life as how we wish it could be.

NOTES 2. faithful 忠実な 11. overwhelmed 圧倒される 12. intensify 強まる 12. in particular 特に 20. flying ace 撃墜王、空の勇士 21. strikes his fancy 想像力のおもむくままに 24. embody 体現する 25. one's own terms 自分の決定に基づいて

Comprehension

Circle the best choice.

1. Which sentence best describes the relationship between Charlie Brown and Snoopy?
   a. They are friends but see their relationship very differently.
   b. It is a typical one between dog and owner.
   c. Charlie Brown is the master and Snoopy his obedient pet.

2. Charlie Brown often feels __________.
   a. well adjusted in society
   b. overwhelmed by society
   c. free from worries

3. Which of the following does NOT apply to Snoopy's approach to life?
   a. imaginative and creative
   b. carefree and positive
   c. passive and reserved

4. Which sentence best summarizes the main idea of the essay?
   a. The Charlie Brown-Snoopy relationship stands for two contrasting approaches to life.
   b. We should all live as freely as Snoopy does.
   c. Friendship is one of the most important things in life.

Think It Over

Q. What do you expect your friends to do when you are feeling down or are having trouble?

Q. What is a stereotype? How do stereotypes come into being? What are some of the more common stereotypes that you know of?

COFFEE BREAK

Lucy's football trick ①

目は心の窓？

Can you really tell what people are going to do by watching their eyes? This brings to mind the old proverb, "The eyes are the windows of the soul." It sounds so true, but is it? Charlie Brown always believes what Lucy says and thinks that this time, he might actually kick the football if only he can keep his eyes on hers ...

Not again!　もうやだよ！
Over here!　こっちよ（こっちに来て）！
What you really mean ~　ほんとは～するつもりなんだろう。
pull away　引っこめる
tip　良いヒント、秘訣
should have thought ~　～について考えておくべきだった
universe　宇宙

Search and Circle: Who's Who?

Find these *Peanuts* characters in the "Search and Circle" puzzle below.
(Hint: Look in all directions — right to left, left to right, up and down, diagonally.)

The little red-haired ____________________.

Charlie ____________________.

Peppermint ____________________.

The girl who runs the psychiatry stand is ____________________.

Charlie Brown's sister is ____________________.

The beagle in *Peanuts* is ____________________.

Lucy's brother is ____________________.

U	G	I	R	L	S
B	R	O	W	N	A
L	A	S	O	B	L
U	E	O	H	F	L
C	P	A	T	T	Y
Y	S	U	N	I	L

LESSON 4

Menu

- Come on, Charlie Brown ...
- *Peanuts* as a Social Group

Cartoon 1

Read and enjoy this comic strip.

Setting the Scene

Charlie Brown is especially nervous on the pitcher's mound today because the little red-haired girl has come to watch the game. He longs to impress her with a great pitching performance, but, oh, no! He cannot stop shaking ...

赤毛の女の子が試合を観に来ているのでピッチャー・マウンドのチャーリー・ブラウンはひどく緊張してしまっています。良いプレーを見せて何とか好印象を与えたいけれど、でもこんな時にかぎって！ 緊張のあまり震えがとまらなくなっちゃった…

Guess the Words

Complete these words that are related to "sports and games."

ma__ch　　fa__r p__ay　　tou__nam__nt

comp__tit__on　　riv__l　　h__me (aw__y) game

Everyday Expressions

Read and memorize these expressions and sentences.

❶ be impressed with

I *am* very *impressed with* her sense of humor.

❷ take someone home

It's getting late, so let me *take you home*.

❸ go to bed

I was surfing the internet for hours last night, so I *went to bed* pretty late.

Mini-Application

Translate this sentence into English using the words and expressions above.

彼らは宿命のライバルだが、彼らのフェアープレイ精神にはすごく感動した。
（宿命のライバル＝ bitter rivals）

Verb Review

Come on, Charlie Brown...

さあ、チャーリー・ブラウン ...

赤毛の女の子にいいところを見せたい！ 緊張のあまり野球の試合中に震えだしてしまったチャーリー・ブラウン。さあ、家まで送ってあげる。マウンドにかけよったライナスが手を差しのべます。come は、“やって来る”“ある状態に到達する”が基本イメージです。come to an end（終わる）come to the conclusion（結論に達する）などの他に、come to know, come to realize など come to に動詞が続くと、ある時間を経て“～するようになる”という意味になります。

Listen and Repeat

11

Repeat these sentences after the audio.

1. Come and see me again.
2. I gradually came to know him better.
3. I came across a good recipe for lasagna.
4. The total comes to $60 dollars.
5. Where do you come from?
6. How come you didn't go to the concert?

Listen and Write

12

Listen and fill in the blanks in these short dialogues.

1. W: Hurry! Your favorite (   ) is coming up next.
   M: OK, I'm coming right now (   ) the popcorn.

2. W: Professor Smith, I don't have much (   ) in my term paper.
   M: Well, if you revise it (   ), I'm sure it'll come out fine.

3. W: (   ) plagiarism from other sources is so important.
   M: Definitely. If you steal someone else's writing, your academic (   ) can come to an end.

4. M: You (   ) so many applications for the position.
   W: Yes, but after screening them all, we came to the conclusion that this (   ) was the best candidate.

Cartoon 2

Read and enjoy this comic strip.

* short essay　短いレポート
* words ever spoken　今まで話された言葉の中で
* to feed　食事を与える

学校からの帰り道、サリーは宿題の意味がよくわかりません。ライナスとルーシーは説明してあげますが、スヌーピーの見解では…

Reading

13

***Peanuts* as a Social Group**

ピーナッツの漫画では、学校の先生や両親など大人の姿は全く描かれていません。チャーリー・ブラウンたちは大人のかかえるような悩みも持ちますが、同時に彼らは社会の中で彼らだけの独自の世界を形成しているのです。

No adult ever appears in *Peanuts*. Every now and then, a strip refers to a generic adult character such as a teacher or parent, but none ever shows up as a figure drawn in the strip. Although Charlie Brown and the other children have the same worries and problems as grown-ups, they shape their own world as a small social group within and yet apart from the world of adults.

Seeing the children of *Peanuts* as a distinct social group reminds us that although we enter and leave the world alone in birth and death, we are seldom alone in life. We belong to groups that integrate us into society. The family is fundamental to this process, but other groups based on age, gender, education, occupation, and common interests also play important roles. Among the Masai of Africa, for example, boys are separated from their families at an early age and start living together in a special house where they learn the skills and knowledge they will need to become responsible men. Undergoing various rites of passage during the time they spend together as a group promotes their solidarity as a new generation of village leaders.

In American colleges, there are groups of students approximately the same age who set themselves apart from the rest of the college's social world. They eat, sleep, and study together in large off-campus houses with unique names comprising two or three letters from the Greek alphabet. They call themselves "brothers" or "sisters." Their behavior and practices, many of which are secretive, unite them and create ties that can last a lifetime. These groups, called fraternities for the men and sororities for the women, are an important component of their college social life.

As a comic strip, *Peanuts*' focus on the social world of children is unique. But around the globe there are many cultural examples of young people living and shaping their lives together through the values of harmony, companionship, and common life experiences.

NOTES 4. shape 形成する　10. the Masai ケニア・タンザニアに住むマサイ族　12. rites of passage 通過儀礼
13. solidarity 結束、連帯　17. off-campus オフ・キャンパスの、大学の敷地外の（↔ on campus）

Comprehension

Circle the best choice.

1. No adults appear in *Peanuts* because __________.
   a. it is intended for child readers only
   b. the characters never behave or think as adults do
   c. the characters create their own world separate from that of adults

2. Many social groups are formed based upon __________.
   a. age or common interests
   b. occupation
   c. both a. and b.

3. Fraternities are __________.
   a. groups of male university students who do almost everything together while in college
   b. groups of male students who take the same college classes
   c. seminars of male students organized by their professors

4. Which sentence best summarizes the main idea of the essay?
   a. Social groups in traditional societies are not so well formed as those in modern societies.
   b. Members of social groups share experiences and foster enduring ties.
   c. The family is more important than any other group.

Think It Over

Q. What social groups do you belong to both in and outside of school? What kind of people are attracted to these groups?

Q. Are there close-knit social groups of young people in Japan like those of the Masai in Africa and the fraternities and sororities in American colleges?

LESSON 5

Menu

- You got it!
- Schroeder the Music Lover

Cartoon 1

Read and enjoy this comic strip.

Setting the Scene

Lucy shouts that she doesn't want to play right field. She hates standing out in the rain. Charlie Brown tries to motivate her by reminding her of her love for Schroeder, the team's catcher.

ライトの守備なんてイヤ！ ルーシーは叫んでいます。雨の中で立ったまま野球をするのなんて大嫌い！ チャーリー・ブラウンは何とかルーシーをやる気にさせようとしています。ほら、キミの好きなシュローダーが捕手をしてるじゃないか。

Guess the Words

Complete these words that are related to "love."

af__ect__on　　ca__ing　　fo__dn__ss

d__ar　　pas__ion　　ende__rm__nt

Everyday Expressions

Read and memorize these expressions and sentences.

❶ in the rain

I was caught *in the rain*.

❷ hate

I *hate* to say this, but she's not the singer she used to be.

❸ love

Give my *love* to Chris.

I *love* your suit. Where did you get it?

Mini-Application

Translate this sentence into English using the words and expressions above.

はじめはこの仕事が好きじゃなかったけれど、今は大好きになった。

Verb Review

You **got** it!

そのとおり！

野球の試合は好きじゃないけど、シュローダーがキャッチャーなら頑張ろうっと！ get はピーナッツの漫画でも日常生活でも最もよく使われる動詞の一つで、お金や車のような実際の物から、時間やハートやチャンスなど目に見えないものまで “手に入れる” “得る” イメージです。get の後に warm, better など形容詞が来ると become（～になる）という意味です。特に口語では get lost（迷う）get used（慣れる）get tired（疲れる）get involved（関わる）など動詞の過去分詞形とともに使う例も多くあります。また誰かに何かをさせる、してもらう、という使役の意味も表現できます。

Listen and Repeat

14

Repeat these sentences after the audio.

1. It's getting late.
2. Let's get together sometime.
3. I got my computer fixed.
4. "Jane, the phone's ringing." "OK, I'll get it."
5. I'll get her to sign the form.

Listen and Write

15

Listen and fill in the blanks in these short dialogues.

1. M: When did you get (   ) from Paris?
   W: Just last night. It'll take me a while to get over my (   ) lag, I'm sure.

2. W: Professor Smith, I was very (   ) by the results of my last test.
   M: Well, you've just got to work (   ).

3. W: I've just gotten a master's (   ) in history. I did it all (   ).
   M: Good for you! Congratulations!

4. W: You seem to have gotten (   ) to graduate school life quite quickly.
   M: Yes, and I am getting (   ) well with my professors, too.

5. M: How can I get her to come to the (   )?
   W: If I were you, I would (   ) her and tell her how much you want her to be there.

6. M: I'm in a panic. I've still got so much (   ) to do.
   W: Next time, you should (   ) working on your assignments as soon as you get them.

Cartoon 2

Read and enjoy this comic strip.

❶

＊ be restricted to ~　～に制限される
＊ Did you know that?　わかってるの？

❷

❸

❹

一方的にシュローダーに熱をあげているルーシーですが、彼の頭の中はいつもベートーヴェンのことばかり。腹がたったルーシーは思わず叫んでしまいます。

Reading

16

Schroeder the Music Lover

クラシック音楽愛好家、シュローダー。ピアノに向かう彼にはルーシーは目に入りません。シュローダーにとってのベートーヴェンの演奏がそうであるように、音楽は個人の性格やグループとしてのアイデンティティを表現するものの一つでしょう。

The foremost—perhaps only—classical music lover in *Peanuts* is Schroeder. No matter how hard Lucy tries to get his attention, Schroeder always ignores her by playing Beethoven on his toy piano. Schroeder's deep love of Beethoven often leads Lucy to insult the composer in fits of jealousy. For Schroeder, however, music is more than just a way to ignore Lucy or even a hobby. It is something that distinguishes him from the other *Peanuts* characters. In other words, music expresses his personality and identity, allowing Schroeder to be cool, aloof, and calm.

As it is in Schroeder's case, one basic function of music is the expression of identity, both for the individual and the group. Walk into any large music store in Tokyo, for example, and you will see many music lovers looking at and listening to different CDs based on their personal preferences. Some listen to the latest hit songs while others prefer jazz, classical, or world music. Picture this. A father and his teenage son visit such a store together. The son immediately heads for the floor that sells the trendiest pops, while the father goes to the classical section to seek out music that is two or three centuries old.

Music not only expresses individual identity, but it also reflects group identity. We associate the sounds of Beethoven with Schroeder. But for anyone who has watched the classic *Peanuts* animated television specials, the soft sounds of Vince Guaraldi's jazz piano convey the identities of the entire group of diverse characters—from gentle and shy Charlie Brown to crabby Lucy. Of course, the love of Schroeder's life—Beethoven—can also express group identity. Every December, as the New Year approaches, Japanese music lovers gather in different venues to listen to live performances of Beethoven's Ninth Symphony. At these concerts, professionals and amateurs, men and women, young and old, can enjoy singing the final choral movement, "Ode to Joy," together. In this way, Beethoven's music represents for many Japanese their shared hope for a happy and joyous New Year.

I'll bet Schroeder would love to be in Japan during the final month of the year. That is, of course, if Lucy did not accompany him. She would just get in the way of Schroeder's passion and enjoyment.

NOTES 4. in fits of jealousy ジェラシーから　7. aloof 近づき難い　17. Vince Guaraldi サンフランシスコ出身のジャズ・ミュージシャン。代表作にアルバム *A Charlie Brown Christmas* がある。　21. venues 開催地　23. Ode to Joy「歓喜に寄す」（ベートーヴェン第９の合唱部分）　26. get in the way 邪魔をする

Comprehension

Circle the best choice.

1. For Schroeder, music is _________.
   a. nothing but a hobby
   b. the expression of his personal identity
   c. a way to become a great composer like Beethoven

2. Which of these would the father mentioned in this essay likely buy at the music store?
   a. the latest hip-hop record
   b. a contemporary world music CD
   c. a Mozart or Bach recording

3. Which of the following is true concerning Beethoven's Ninth Symphony?
   a. The final movement is for orchestra only.
   b. It can only be heard on New Year's Day.
   c. For many Japanese, it symbolizes shared hope.

4. Which sentence best expresses the main idea of the essay?
   a. Both individuals and groups can define their identity through certain kinds of music.
   b. Music should be pursued by experts and professionals only.
   c. Schroeder is even more passionate about Beethoven's Ninth Symphony than most Japanese.

Think It Over

Q. What kind of music do you like most? When do you like to listen to your favorite music?

Q. Besides music, what other ways do we have for expressing our identity and personality?

LESSON 6

Menu

- Why don't you try taking ...
- Girls in *Peanuts*

Cartoon 1

Read and enjoy this comic strip.

Setting the Scene

Charlie Brown is lonely again—or still! Lucy suggests that he take dance lessons. But Charlie Brown being Charlie Brown, he soon lets his anxieties take over. What if no one wants to dance with him? Then what? Lucy has an answer, though not a very kindly one.

また淋しくなってしまったチャーリー・ブラウン。それならダンスを習ったら？とアドバイスをするルーシー。でも彼の不安はさらなる不安をよびます。もし誰もボクとダンスしてくれなかったら？ もちろん、答えを知っているのはルーシーですが…

Guess the Words

Complete these words that are related to "lessons."

co__rse　　works__op　　s__min__r

cr__dit　　regi__trat__on

Everyday Expressions

Read and memorize these expressions and sentences.

❶ Why don't you ...?

Why don't you ask your adviser about the course requirements?

❷ What if ...

What if the computer had never been invented? What would life be like without it?

❸ how to ...

I have never sent an e-mail with a document attached. Would you show me *how to* do it?

Mini-Application

Translate this sentence into English using the words and expressions above.

科目の履修のしかたを教えてもらうのには留学生のアドバイザーに聞いてみたら？

（留学生のためのアドバイザー＝ foreign student adviser）

Verb Review

Try **taking** dance lessons.
ダンスのレッスンを取ってみたら？

take は“何かをつかみ取る”“何かを選び取って自分と共にどこかへ持ってゆく”という動作が基本イメージです。ダンスレッスンを習ったり学校の科目を履修するのも take です。take into account（考慮する）take charge of（担当する）などの慣用的な表現、take out（誰かを連れ出す、お金を引き出す、ファーストフード店での持ち帰り）take off（離陸する、衣服や靴を脱ぐ）のように意味が多岐にわたるイディオムもあります。また Take your time.（急がなくてもいいよ）のように時間やお金や労力が“かかる”“必要とされる”のも take です。それぞれの例文の中でニュアンスをつかみましょう。

Listen and Repeat

17

Repeat these sentences after the audio.

1. May I take your coat?
2. Let's take a look at this DVD.
3. You should take a rest.
4. Don't take it so seriously.
5. Take good care of yourself.
6. I am taking five courses this semester.

Listen and Write

18

Listen and fill in the blank in these short dialogues.

1. M: May I (   ) to Professor Smith, please?
   W: He is in a committee (   ) right now. Can I take a message?

2. M: How about (   ) by Clark's Diner for a bite?
   W: Maybe (   ) time. I've got a lot of chores to take care of.

3. M: This (   ) is taking forever.
   W: Here, (   ) me help you out with it.

4. M: The homecoming (   ) will take place at the Alumni Center on Saturday (   ). Will you be able to help out with the catering?
   W: I will if I can take some (   ) off from my studies.

Cartoon 2

Read and enjoy this comic strip.

❶

* organize　整える、編成する
* bring over　連れて行く、率いて行く
* slaughter　（スポーツの試合で）完敗させる
* mangle　徹底的に破壊する
* stomp on　踏みつける
* crush　圧倒する、押しつぶす
* trample into　踏みつける、ひどい扱いをする

❷

❸

❹

運動神経抜群の女のコ、ペパーミント パティが自信たっぷりに宣戦布告しています。来週の試合まであと少し。チャーリー・ブラウンはすっかり怖くなって…

Reading

19

Girls in *Peanuts*

ピーナッツの女の子たちはとってもアクティブ。性別は２種類しかないけれど、男らしさや女らしさ、そして男女の役割分担は文化によって多様性があるようです。

Masculinity is traditionally defined as comprising qualities like competitiveness, athleticism, and aggressiveness. Thus, we may be surprised to find that in *Peanuts*, these attributes most often apply to girls rather than boys. Lucy is bossy and loud. She strives to make money from various enterprises, the most famous of which is her psychiatry stand. Peppermint Patty, meanwhile, is the most competitive and skillful athlete among all the children in *Peanuts*. She is, to use a term usually applied to boys, a classic "jock": a terrible student but a great athlete. Looking at Lucy and Peppermint Patty, in contrast to the sensitive and gentle Charlie Brown and Linus, for example, we might rightly ask, Aren't stereotypical gender roles reversed in *Peanuts*?

Unlike the word "sex," which refers to males or females from a strictly biological aspect, "gender" is culturally defined. As the imaginary world of *Peanuts* indicates, gender roles are not fixed and show great diversity throughout the world. In some societies, gender roles are very flexible and in others highly differentiated. Many westernized societies exemplify the former. Participation in work, sports, and education is open to all regardless of sex. Boys and girls study together in primary and secondary public schools. Women sit in boardrooms and work on assembly lines. Female sports—from skating to soccer—are very popular. Perhaps because *Peanuts*' creator, Charles Schulz, grew up in such a society—the U.S.—he was able to twist or manipulate traditional notions of gender for the sake of humor. Indeed, his 50-year professional career paralleled the rise of feminism, the expansion of female sports in schools and universities, and the increase in the number of female college graduates and professionals. These social changes broadened the social roles and life choices available to women in many countries in Western Europe, East Asia including Japan, and North America.

In this light, we can see Lucy and Peppermint Patty not just as humorous characters, but also as trendsetters. In the sixties and early seventies, when most girls were content to dream only of things like marriage, the girls of *Peanuts* were already running businesses—and running circles around boys on the athletic field.

NOTES 1. comprising 構成する、含む　2. attributes 性質、特質　3. strive 努力する、熱心にする　13. differentiate 分化する　15. boardrooms（会社などの）会議室　18. manipulate 巧みに扱う　23. in this light このような見方をすれば　24. trendsetters 流行を創り出す人　24. content 満足する

Comprehension

Circle the best choice.

1. Which of these qualities pertain to the girls in *Peanuts*?
   a. ambitious and energetic
   b. docile and passive
   c. quiet and submissive

2. Which of the following is true according to the essay?
   a. "Gender" and "sex" can be used interchangeably.
   b. What is feminine or masculine is culturally defined.
   c. Traditional gender roles are well defined in *Peanuts*.

3. Charles Schulz's career coincided with the advance of ________.
   a. the feminism movement in the U.S.
   b. co-ed education in American colleges
   c. both a. and b.

4. Which sentence best summarizes the main idea of the essay?
   a. The boys and girls in *Peanuts* do not get along because of their gender differences.
   b. Typical gender roles are often reversed in *Peanuts*.
   c. Charles Schulz created *Peanuts* only because he wanted to promote feminism.

Think It Over

Q. In Japan, are there any occupations or workplaces that are differentiated according to sex?

Q. In Japan, what things or behaviors are considered feminine and what things masculine?

COFFEE BREAK

Lucy' football trick ②

すべてのものには時がある？

Lucy quotes a famous passage from the Bible that says that there is an appropriate time in life for everything. This means different things to different people. Charlie Brown thinks that now is the time to kick the football. But, of course, for Lucy, now is the time to...

Ecclesiastes （旧約聖書の）伝道の書（「コヘレトの言葉」とも言われる）
season ここでは何かをするのにふさわしい時、の意。
plant 植える
pluck 刈り取る、（花などを）摘む
mourn 嘆き悲しむ、喪に服する

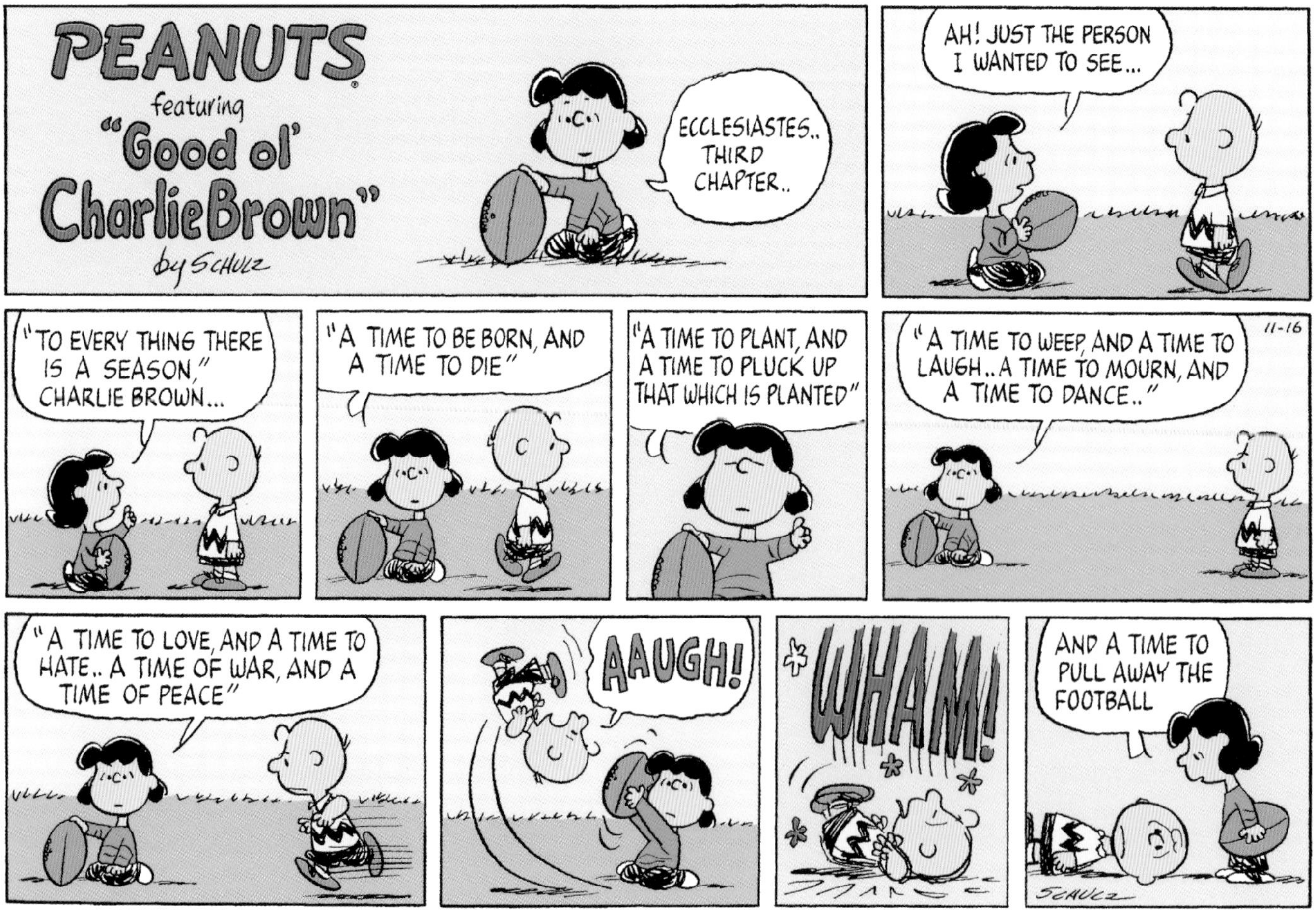

Search and Circle: Personal Touch!

Find the qualities in the "Search and Circle" puzzle below that apply to these characters.

Charlie Brown is ____________________ and ____________________.

Lucy is ____________________ and ____________________.

Schroeder is ____________________ and ____________________.

Linus is ____________________ and ____________________.

N	E	G	A	S	Q
I	Y	E	J	H	U
K	I	N	D	Y	I
A	C	T	I	V	E
C	A	L	M	C	T
V	M	E	A	N	E

LESSON 7

Menu

- How I can put the blame ...
- Sally and her Legal Beagle

Cartoon 1

Read and enjoy this comic strip.

Setting the Scene

Sally is in trouble at school—again! She made fun of her class field trip, which upset her teacher. Is there any way she can get herself out of trouble? Yes, she thinks. Why not find a way to blame it all on Charlie Brown?

サリーはまた学校で問題を起こしてしまいました。フィールドトリップについて文句を言ったので、先生を怒らせてしまったのです。どうすればこの状況を打開できるかしら？ そうだ、サリーは思いつきます。兄貴のチャーリー・ブラウンのせいにしちゃえば…

Guess the Words

Complete these words that are related to "teacher."

ed__cator　　instr__ct__r　　le__tur__r

pr__fes__or　　Te__ching Assist__nt (TA)　　m__ntor

Everyday Expressions

Read and memorize these expressions and sentences.

❶ be (get) mad at ...

I regret teasing him so much. He really *got mad at* me.

❷ call

I wouldn't *call* him a genius, but he is really smart.

❸ figure out ...

I can't *figure out* how to put this bookcase together.

Mini-Application

Translate this sentence into English using the words and expressions above.

もしこの新製品を何と呼ぶか私が考えなければ、上司は怒るだろうな。

(新製品＝ new product、上司＝ boss)

Verb Review

Put the blame on ...
…のせいにする

先生を怒らせてしまったけど、兄貴のチャーリー・ブラウンのせいにしてしまえば…サリーは責任のがれを考えています。put の基本は “手を使って何かをある場所に置く、入れる、付ける” というニュアンスですが、日本語の “置く” とは少し違って、お金を預金したり名前を名簿やリストに載せたりという場合にも使います。 put on は “～のせいにする” という以外にも、服を着る、電気をつけるなどの意味があります。状況によってふさわしい日本語を当てはめましょう。

Listen and Repeat

Repeat these sentences after the audio. 20

1. I usually put a little milk in my coffee.
2. I can't put up with her any more.
3. Where shall we put up the Christmas tree?
4. The police put down the riot.
5. We had to put off the party until next weekend.
6. It's quite cold out today, so you should put your jacket on.

Listen and Write

Listen and fill in the blanks in these short dialogues. 21

1. W: You look (   ). You've been (   ) too hard lately.
   M: I know. The (   ) schedule is putting a lot of pressure on me.

2. W: Where did you put your (   ) phone?
   M: I'm not sure ... maybe in my (   ).

3. W: What are your (   ) as a student worker in the library?
   M: Well, they're pretty (   ) ... putting books back on the bookshelves, mainly.

4. M: Hello. Would you put me (   ) to the admissions office, please?
   W: The line's busy right now. I'll put you on (   ).

Cartoon 2

Read and enjoy this comic strip.

❶

＊ sue　訴える
＊ attorney　弁護士
＊ this case　この訴訟、この判例
＊ bother　悩ます

❷

❸

❹

兄貴のチャーリー・ブラウンに宿題をやらせようとして強硬手段に出たサリー。でも弁護士役のスヌーピーはこの訴訟を扱えるのでしょうか…

Reading

22

Sally and her Legal Beagle

宿題を手伝ってくれないなら、チャーリー・ブラウンを訴えると迫る勉強嫌いのサリー。サリーの後ろに控えているのは弁護士に扮したスヌーピーです。法廷で？ それとも歌で？ トラブルの解決方法は社会によってさまざまですが…

Sally despises any kind of responsibility—especially homework. She never hesitates to threaten her brother Charlie Brown with “legal action” for not helping her with her assignments. At such times, she gets Snoopy to act as her “attorney.”

When you have trouble with a family member, friend, neighbor, or colleague at work, how do you react or deal with it? Get angry and start shouting? Put your hand out to shake hands and try to reconcile with the person? Apologize or ask for an apology? We must all live together, and for any society to function well, there must be order. Rules, mores, and customs are some of the ways that society encourages appropriate behavior in people in order to maintain social harmony. Still, each of us is an individual with a separate will and different needs that sometimes clash with those of other individuals. When such clashes occur in a large, complex society like the United States, for example, a formalized system of law is used to determine who is at fault. This legal system is so complex that it requires highly trained judges and lawyers to make it work. Juries, selected from among ordinary citizens, listen to a case and then try to reach an agreement, or verdict. The goal is to determine as objectively as possible whether an individual is guilty or innocent, at fault or not.

In traditional, smaller-scale societies, law tends to be less formal. The goal typically is not to penalize an individual, but simply to restore social harmony. Among the Inuit of Northern Canada, for instance, a “song duel” has traditionally been used as a means of settling disputes. Two Inuits with mutual grievances publicly insult each other with songs specifically composed for the occasion. Spectators determine the outcome with applause that shows their approval of one singer’s songs over those of the other. With this approval, the dispute is considered over. The loser must accept the decision or leave the group. Either way, social harmony is restored.

Of course, Sally is more interested in getting her own way than in promoting harmony. Will she ever come up with a solution for her homework “problem” other than “suing” her brother? Probably not. We all know that the only real solution is for her to take responsibility and study harder. But try telling that to Sally!

NOTES 7. mores 道徳観　17. penalize 有罪とする、罰する　18. duel 競争、腕比べ　19. grievances 不平・苦情　20. outcome 結果　27. But try telling that to Sally! = But you will never be able to convince Sally of that.

Comprehension

Circle the best choice.

1. Which of these encourage people to behave properly?
   a. customs and mores
   b. regulations and rules
   c. both a. and b.

2. Juries are __________.
   a. groups of professional people who are experts at legal issues
   b. ordinary people selected from among a country's or state's citizens
   c. individuals who may or may not be guilty of a crime

3. Among the Inuit, which method is used to solve disagreements?
   a. a song contest
   b. taking a person to court
   c. paying money to the victim

4. Which sentence best summarizes the main idea of the essay?
   a. Since it is wrong to penalize others, we should learn forgiveness.
   b. The best way to solve our problems is to threaten legal action.
   c. Different societies create different ways of solving disputes between people.

Think It Over

Q. When you have trouble with your friends, how do you usually handle it?

Q. Are you the kind of person who always avoids trouble with others, or the kind who, when necessary, stands up and defends yourself even if it causes more trouble?

LESSON 8

Menu

- Are you all set ...?
- Linus's Security Blanket

Cartoon 1

Read and enjoy this comic strip.

Setting the Scene

Linus obviously hasn't studied for today's test and is really worried about it. But once he finds out it's a true or false test, and not an essay test ... well, that's a different thing altogether.

試験だけど、明らかに準備不足…朝から試験のことが心配なライナスです。記述式の試験だったら自信がないし困っちゃう。でも○×式なら、それなら話は別かも…

Guess the Words

Complete these words that are related to "essay."

pa__er co__pos__tion th__sis

ar__icle dis__ertati__n

Everyday Expressions

Read and memorize these expressions and sentences.

❶ What a ...

What a feast! It all looks delicious!

❷ take a test ...

Taking a test always makes me anxious.

❸ have the wind at your back

Since finding this job, I really feel I *have the wind at my back*.

Mini-Application

Translate this sentence into English using the words and expressions above.

何ていう一日だろう！ テストも受けなきゃいけないし、レポートも２つ出さなきゃいけないなんて！ （テストを受ける = take a test、レポートを出す = submit papers）

Verb Review

Are you all set for the test?
テストの準備できた？

朝、通学途中のふたりはテストについて話しています。この場面の Are you all set? は、準備が完了した？という意味です。外出する際の“用意できた？”という意味や、No thanks. I am all set で、食事のおかわりなどを勧められて“もう十分なのでけっこうです”という意味にもなります。set は“置く”が基本の意味ですが、ほとんどどこにでも置ける put と違って、“あるべき状態や場所におさまる、設定する、据える”というニュアンスです。

Listen and Repeat

23

Repeat these sentences after the audio.

1. He set the poem to music.
2. Make sure you set your alarm.
3. He set off for Paris last week.
4. I've set my sights on becoming a voice actor.
5. Will you help me set the table?
6. You must set realistic goals for yourself.

Listen and Write

24

Listen and fill in the blanks in these short dialogues.

1. M: Customer service. How may I (　　　　　) you?
   W: I (　　　　　) someone to set up the internet on my (　　　　　) for me.

2. W: Would you (　　　　　) for any dessert?
   M: No, thanks. I'm all set. Dinner was delicious.

3. W: I'm sorry I (　　　　　) on the exam, Professor Smith.
   M: I have no (　　　　　) but to fail you. This will set an example for the rest of the class.

4. W: That new TV (　　　　　) is set in the 18th century.
   M: That makes sense. I thought the dialogue sounded a (　　　　　) different.

Cartoon 2

Read and enjoy this comic strip.

❶

* I am going to be what?　僕が何だって？
* enter ~　～を登場させる、出品する
* school science fair　学校の科学展（生徒が独自の科学作品や研究を発表する）
* series of tests　一連のテスト
* insecure　不安な

❷

❸

❹

ライナスがいつも抱えている大事な毛布。この毛布がどんな安心感を与えているのかしら？　そうだ、科学的に実験してみよう！ルーシーの思いつきにライナスは…

Reading

25

Linus's Security Blanket

ライナスと彼に安心感を与えている毛布を科学の実験台にしてみよう！ ルーシーのこの提案を聞いただけで、ライナスは突然不安になってしまいました。ピーナッツの漫画をきっかけに、心理学用語のみならずアメリカ英語として定着したセキュリティーブランケットとは一体どんなものでしょうか？

Charles Schulz's iconic image of Linus depicts him with his eyes closed, sucking his thumb, and holding his blanket to his cheek. As long as his blanket is close at hand, Linus has the peace of mind and strength of heart to face daily problems and challenges, especially his sister Lucy's crabbiness. Like Linus, we all appreciate a sense of security. Charlie Brown once described what makes him feel secure: falling asleep at night in the backseat of the warm family car as his dad drives him and his family home. This is the kind of comforting childhood memory that many of us share. Of course, when we grow up, the privilege of holding on to such a simple sense of security ends. As adults, not only are we doomed to sit in the driver's seat, but we must also face "adult" problems like jobs, mortgages, raising children, and taking care of aging parents. From childhood to adulthood we are always in need of a "security blanket" of some sort.

Through Linus, Charles Schulz popularized the term "security blanket" so that it came to mean any item that provides us with psychological comfort and a sense of serenity. We even use "security blanket" as a metaphor to describe the comfort we gain from such human relationships as a loving spouse or caring friend. The term most specifically denotes the everyday objects many toddlers hold on to—stuffed animals, dolls, and yes, just like Linus, blankets. These objects help children deal with stress when they experience fear, loss, or anger. Most children lose their dependence on these objects by the time they enter elementary school. But much later on, as we enter our "golden years," we may well embrace other objects. For example, elderly people, particularly those living alone or in nursing homes, find that pets such as small dogs or cats—or, these days, even robots—are very helpful in making them feel happier and more secure.

Throughout our lives, from childhood to adulthood, and on into old age, we all hope for peace and happiness. Fulfillment of these hopes, of course, is never guaranteed. But like Linus, we can keep the things we most value close to us—a blanket, a pet, a friend—and gain a sense of security that allows us to better cope with life's vicissitudes.

NOTES 1. depict 描写する　8. doom 運命づける　9. mortgages 住宅ローン　13. serenity 落ち着き　19. "golden years" = the time after one's retirement　26. cope with 上手く対処する　26. vicissitudes（通常複数形で）人生の試練、紆余曲折

Comprehension

Circle the best choice.

1. Charlie Brown feels most secure when _________.
   a. his parents come to pick him up at school
   b. he is playing with other kids
   c. he is sleeping in the backseat of the family car

2. When you become an adult, _________.
   a. you must face problems that only grown-ups have
   b. you do not need a security blanket any longer because you are totally independent
   c. you will have more social and work problems than personal problems

3. In the essay, which of the following is NOT mentioned as an example a security blanket?
   a. a friend or an important human relationship
   b. a luxurious and expensive material item
   c. dolls and stuffed animals

4. Which sentence best summarizes the main idea of the essay?
   a. Regardless of age, a “security blanket” of some sort is essential for psychological stability.
   b. Holding on to a security blanket is a sign of immaturity and childishness.
   c. If only Linus were less insecure and more emotionally stable!

Think It Over

Q. Did you have a “security blanket” when you were a child? How about now?

Q. When did you feel most secure when you were a child?

LESSON 9

Menu

- Why can't you see that?
- Crabby Lucy

Cartoon 1

Read and enjoy this comic strip.

Setting the Scene

As usual, crabby Lucy is mad at her brother Linus. Linus, clutching his security blanket, sucking his thumb, quietly ignores her shouts and accusations. Baby brother Rerun comes up and asks if they are fighting. Linus tells his brother that only one of them is fighting, as usual!

ルーシーはいつものように弟のライナスにガミガミ文句を言っています。でもライナスは彼のおきまりの毛布を抱えたまま、指しゃぶりをしてじっとしています。そこへ一番下の弟リランがやってきて、２人はケンカしているの？ と心配そうに尋ねています。ライナスはこう答えます。もちろんケンカしているのは一人だけさ…

Guess the Words

Complete these words that are related to "fighting."

__tt__ck   ins__lt   offe__d

qu__rrel   conf__i__t   a__gue

Everyday Expressions

Read and memorize these expressions and sentences.

❶ all the time

A: My suitcase has not come off the baggage carousel yet.
B: Don't worry. It'll show up eventually. It happens *all the time*.

❷ drive ... crazy

His driving *drives* me *crazy*.

❸ insist on ...

She *insisted on* having her way.

Mini-Application

Translate this sentence into English using the words and expressions above.

上司はいつも自分のやり方ばかり強要してくる。彼との言い争いで私の気はどうかなりそうだ。

Verb Review

Why can't you **see** ...?
どうしてわからないの？

どうしてわたしの言うことがわからないのよ、とルーシーは怒っています。ここでは see は“理解する”という意味で使われています。目に見えるものも見えないものも“わかる”のが see です。また、単に“見る”だけでなく、調べる、観察する、誰かと付き合う（交際する）、医者に診てもらう、など幅広い意味で使います。今回は see を使った決まり文句や表現を学びましょう。

Listen and Repeat

Repeat these sentences after the audio.

26

1. Let me see.
2. I'll see you later.
3. Are you still seeing Jim?
4. Do you see my point?
5. You had better see a doctor.
6. Can you see the difference?

Listen and Write

Listen and fill in the blanks in these short dialogues.

27

1. M: I'd be (　　　　) to come to the (　　　　) and see you off.
   W: Thanks, but I know how busy you are.

2. W: Professor Smith, I'm afraid (　　　　) is not my strongest (　　　　).
   M: I can see that.

3. M: I should have sent in my application (　　　　) earlier. The (　　　　) was yesterday.
   W: See! I told you to (　　　　) an eye on the calendar.

4. W: As far as I can see, this (　　　　) won't work out. We need to think it over.
   M: All right, let's see. How (　　　　) we go about it?

Cartoon 2

Read and enjoy this comic strip.

❶

＊ Get out of ...!!　～からどいて！！
＊ feel sorry for ...　～に同情する
＊ crabbiness　意地悪
＊ vaccine　ワクチン

❷

❸

❹
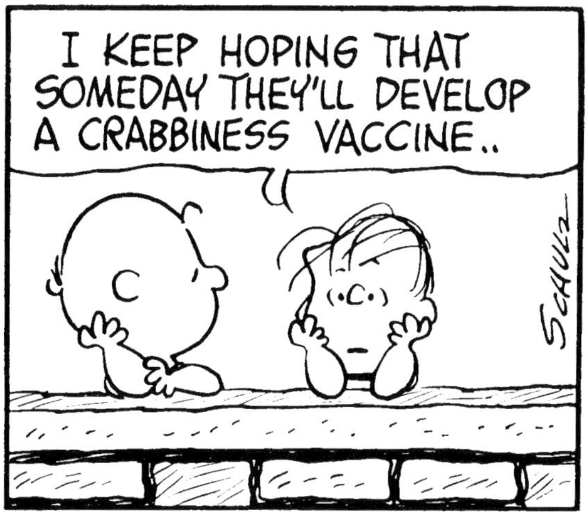

ご機嫌ななめのルーシーに怒鳴られて、唖然とするライナスとチャーリー・ブラウン。そしてライナスはつぶやきます。イジワルの毒に効くワクチンでも開発(develop) されたらなあ…

Reading

28

Crabby Lucy

ピーナッツは可愛く温かいだけの漫画ではありません。強烈な個性の持ち主であるルーシーと彼女をとりまくユーモアが漫画をより魅力的にしています。ユーモアは楽しい時よりも、辛い時や困難に直面した時こそ、その威力を発揮するようです。

Among all the characters in *Peanuts*, Lucy stands out for her meanness and short temper. Charles Schulz once admitted that he did not care for Lucy, but he used her frequently to make the strip funny. Schulz's use of Lucy shows us that an essential element of humor is that it is derived from negative human qualities like meanness and from bad experiences such as failures and misunderstandings. When Lucy tricks Charlie Brown into trying to kick the football, it is funny, not only because he always fails, but because he also fails to see how truly mean Lucy is.

If Charlie Brown's life with Lucy is difficult, just imagine what it would be like to live with Lucy full-time. This is Linus's fate as her little brother. However, in Linus's relationship with Lucy we see another essential element of humor. It can be used as a strategy—or defense mechanism—by people like Linus who find themselves in a weak position in a relationship. Humor functions as a means of distancing ourselves from unpleasantness, enabling us to look at our weaker role more objectively and more philosophically. It also gives us the ability to see the world more realistically and prevents us from feeling totally powerless and self-pitying. To put it another way, humor makes tolerable what is otherwise intolerable. For example, humor has long been a vital part of Native Americans' resistance to white cultural domination and discrimination. This humor can be seen in jokes that poke fun at whites like this one: Question: What did Native Americans say when the Pilgrims landed at Plymouth Rock? Answer: There goes the neighborhood!

Linus uses humor in a similar manner. By ironically hoping that one day a crabbiness vaccine will be developed, he shows Charlie Brown that although Lucy is dominant in their relationship, Linus can tolerate and rise above her crabbiness precisely because he is able to see the humor in it and make fun of it.

By accepting Lucy as she really is, Linus shows us the true value of humor. It allows us to see people as they really are: imperfect, limited, and egocentric. Knowing that we, too, have these defects, we are better able to embrace them in other people. And understanding others is a social skill that is essential for cultivating good human relations.

NOTES 1. stands out 突出している　1. meanness 意地悪　4. derive 引き出す　15. tolerable 耐えられる　17. poke fun at からかう　18. Plymouth Rock ピルグリム・ファーザーズ（Pilgrim Fathers）の最初の上陸地、米国マサチューセッツ州プリマス港にある岩　22. rise above 超越する

Comprehension

Circle the best choice.

1. Which of the following can be applied to Linus?
   a. He sees the humor in his relationship with his sister.
   b. He cannot control himself when his sister gets mad at him.
   c. A vaccine is the only way to help him cope better.

2. Using humor is particularly effective when __________.
   a. we would like to win an argument
   b. we are in a weak position in a relationship
   c. we need to avoid dangerous situations

3. What is meant by the phrase "There goes the neighborhood"?
   a. Go and check out the neighborhood.
   b. That neighborhood no longer exists.
   c. Our new neighbors will ruin everything.

4. Which sentence best expresses the main idea of the essay?
   a. Humor is an effective tool for dealing with difficult situations.
   b. Only people in weak positions can use humor well.
   c. Only educated people truly understand humor.

Think It Over

Q. On what occasions do you use jokes?

Q. What is your favorite comic strip? Why?

COFFEE BREAK

Lucy's football trick ③
リスクを負わないなら…

There is always an ambivalent feeling between challenging oneself and following the status quo. Taking a new step is often a little scary because it means taking a risk. But if you don't dare to try, maybe you won't attain anything. Chances are you'll regret it later on. What are you going to do, Charlie Brown?

go by　時間・年月が過ぎる
risk ~　危険を冒す
the north pole　北極

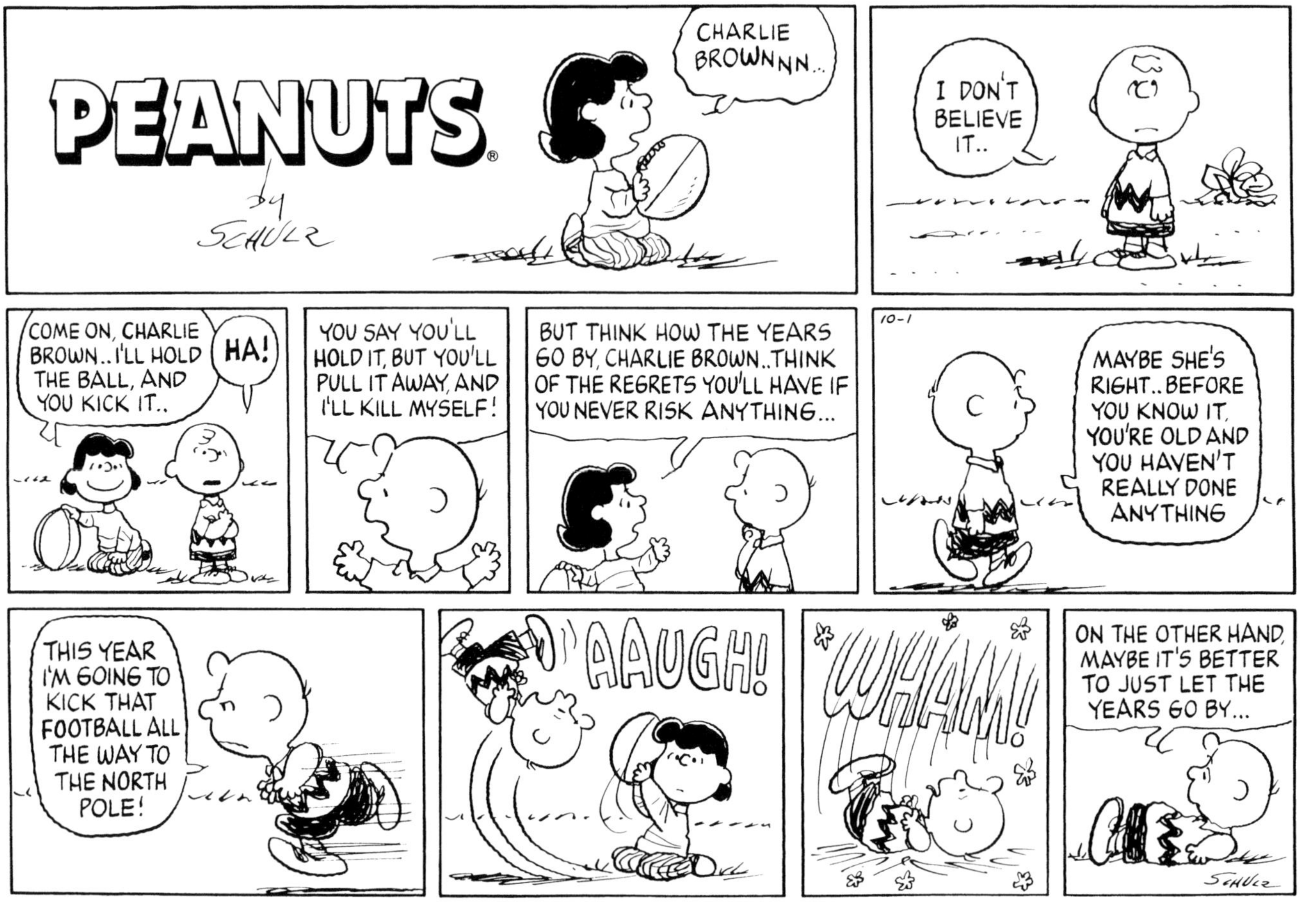

Search and Circle: Experiencing Happiness

'Happiness is a warm puppy' is a famous and beloved line that Charles Schulz first came up with. Find the words in the "Search and Circle" puzzle and complete each sentence below.

Happiness is meeting your ________________.

Happiness is being ________________ at times.

Happiness is having a cup of ________________.

Happiness is finding a shooting ________________ in the sky.

Happiness is making a snowman in ________________.

Happiness is the ________________ of leaves in the fall.

Happiness is reaching your ________________.

Happiness is giving a helping ________________.

Happiness is peace of ________________.

G	O	A	L	F	S
C	O	L	O	R	T
K	A	O	D	I	A
W	I	N	T	E	R
Y	A	E	T	N	S
H	M	I	N	D	T

LESSON 10

Menu

- This very ordinary day could turn out to be ...
- Someday My Great Pumpkin Will Come

Cartoon 1

Read and enjoy this comic strip.

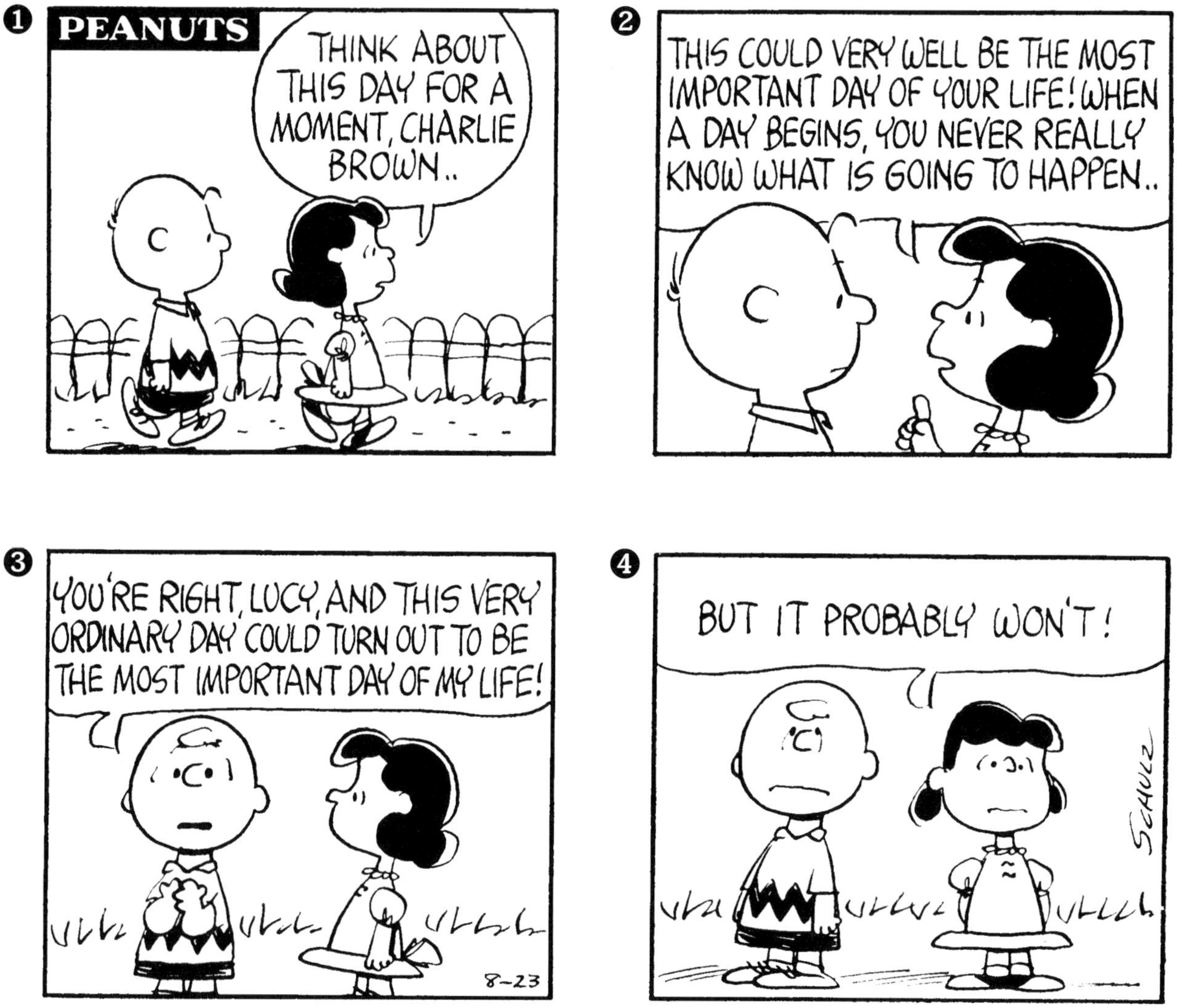

Setting the Scene

Lucy gives Charlie Brown another wonderful piece of advice: live for today because this could be the most important day of your life. And for a moment, at least, Charlie Brown believes that she is actually being kind and thoughtful.

ルーシーは今回もすばらしいアドバイス(！)を授けています。今日一日を生きるのよ、チャーリー・ブラウン。だって、もしかしたら今日が人生で一番大切な一日になるかもしれないの…確かにそうかもしれないとその気になるチャーリー・ブラウンですが…

Guess the Words

Complete these words that are related to "important."

cr__cial　　es__ential　　v__lua__le

s__gnific__nt　　sal__ent

Everyday Expressions

Read and memorize these expressions and sentences.

❶ This could be ...

This could be the best thing that has ever happened to me.

❷ What is going to happen ...?

What is going to happen to the class now that Professor Smith is in the hospital?

❸ ... you're right

Now that I have thought about it, I see that *you're right*.

Mini-Application

Translate this sentence into English using the words and expressions above.

明日何が起こるか、なんてわからない。まさに願っていた通りのことがあるかもしれないよ。

____

Verb Review

... could **turn** out to be the most important day ...
一番大事な一日になるかもしれない…

何でもないように見える一日も、もしかしたら人生で一番大事な日へと変わるかも…ルーシーの教訓はもっともらしく聞こえますね。turn の基本イメージは“転じる”“向きを変える”ですが、turn out（結果として〜になる）turn in（宿題や答案などを提出する）turn up（人や物が現れる・出てくる）など副詞を伴っていろいろな意味に変化します。今回は turn を使ったさまざまな表現を学びましょう。

Listen and Repeat

Repeat these sentences after the audio. 29

1. Turn up the stereo, please.
2. He just turned forty.
3. Jazz turns me on.
4. Please turn off the TV.
5. He turned down my offer.
6. She didn't turn up on time.

Listen and Write

Listen and fill in the blanks in these short dialogues. 30

1. M: Do you know anything about the (   ) of Gettysburg?
   W: It turned the tide of the American (   ) War, didn't it?

2. W: Professor Smith, when should we turn in our (   ) papers?
   M: Right after (   ) break.

3. M: Were you (   ) about your (   )?
   W: I was, but as it turned out, I got an A-.

4. M: Will you (   ) me (   ) Grand Central Station is?
   W: Oh, sure. Turn left at that corner and go (   ) for two blocks.
   You can't miss it.

Cartoon 2

Read and enjoy this comic strip.

❶

* Uh, huh ...　そうなんだ…
* tricks or treats　お菓子をくれなければイタズラするぞ（ハロウィンの夜、近隣の家々を訪ねる時、子供たちがこの決まり文句を言う）
* junk　たわいのない、ガラクタの
* put in a good word　良く言っておいてあげるよ
* doomed　運が尽きる
* pass by　通り過ぎる、素通りする

❷

❸

❹

カボチャ畑に座って、一人カボチャ大王を待つライナス。絶対来てくれると信じているけれど、つい口がすべってしまって…ああ、この一言がカボチャ大王のご機嫌を損ねないといいけれど…

Reading

31

Someday My Great Pumpkin Will Come

ライナスが一年中で一番楽しみにしているハロウィン。カボチャ大王は今年こそ沢山の贈り物を持って会いに来てくれると信じているライナスですが、いつかきっとユートピアのような世界が来ると信じたい気持ちは、誰にでもあるかもしれません。メラネシアのカーゴ・カルト（積荷信仰）もその一つです。

For Linus, the biggest event of the year is Halloween. Every October, he hopes—even believes—that the Great Pumpkin will pop up in his pumpkin patch and bring him presents. As Halloween approaches, Linus tidies up his patch and behaves nicely to everyone in the hope that the Great Pumpkin will choose his patch from which to rise up and fly around the world to deliver toys to all good children. His wish, however, is never realized. Still, Linus never gives up. He sits in his patch waiting faithfully, even missing out on the fun of going out trick-or-treating like all the other kids.

Linus's belief in the Great Pumpkin may seem strange because, unlike Santa Claus, the concept is so unfamiliar to us. Often when something is unfamiliar—like a pumpkin flying in the sky delivering toys—we think it is weird. But when something is familiar like an overweight old man in a red suit climbing down chimneys with a bag full of toys, we accept it as normal. Yet Linus's faith in the Great Pumpkin is not so odd-sounding when we consider its similarity to a religious faith called the Cargo Cult. "Cargo" refers to goods that are transported from place to place on trains and ships, say, and a "cult" is a small, faith-based group. The Cargo Cult spread among the islanders of the southwest Pacific in the early twentieth century after they encountered westerners and modern technology for the first time. This experience prompted them to believe that one day their ancestors would arrive in ships and airplanes and bring them all kinds of luxurious, modern goods like those that the westerners possessed. The islanders hoped that this would balance out their power relations with westerners and usher in a new age of happiness. Similarly, Linus's faith in the Great Pumpkin gives him hope that his friends, and especially his sister Lucy, will no longer tease him but will instead revere him.

Of course, the Pacific islanders' ancestors never came. Linus's Great Pumpkin never comes. Western domination of the islanders continued. Lucy never stops criticizing Linus for his belief. Still, the islanders' and Linus's dream, although never realized, represents a simple but powerful hope most of us hold: that the future promises better days.

NOTES 3. tidies up 整える　12. odd-sounding 風変わりに聞こえる　19. balance out = to make equal　20. usher in 導く、～の到来を告げる　22. revere 尊敬する、崇拝する

Comprehension

Circle the best choice.

1. On Halloween what does Linus do?
   a. He goes out trick-or-treating with his friends.
   b. He waits for the Great Pumpkin in his pumpkin patch.
   c. He distributes toys to neighborhood children.

2. Why does the Great Pumpkin seem weird to us?
   a. Because we are not familiar with the idea.
   b. Because only Linus has ever seen it.
   c. Because Santa Claus is a better idea.

3. What was the main belief of the Cargo Cult?
   a. That western technology was the best in the world.
   b. That one day their ancestors would bring about an ideal world.
   c. That the balance of power with westerners would never change.

4. Which sentence best expresses the main idea of the essay?
   a. Our hopes for a better world can manifest themselves in a variety of ways.
   b. Halloween is as popular as Christmas in the U.S.
   c. Religious faith always grows out of unequal relations.

Think It Over

Q. For you, what would an ideal world be like?

Q. What beliefs did you have as a child that you now no longer hold?

LESSON 11

Menu

- Linus, do me a favor ...
- Good Grief! It's Valentine's Day.

Cartoon 1

Read and enjoy this comic strip.

Setting the Scene

Charlie Brown doesn't have the nerve to approach the little red-haired girl on his own. So he asks Linus to do it for him—but please, he tells Linus, don't let her know that it's me doing the asking. OK, Linus? Please! Oh, no! How humiliating!

気になる彼女は自分のことを気づいてくれたことがあるのかな？ チャーリー・ブラウンは赤毛の女の子が自分のことをどう思っているのか聞き出してきてほしいとライナスに頼んでいます。自分では確かめる勇気がないのです。でもライナスったら！ こっそり聞いてみてって言ったのに…

Guess the Words

Complete these words that are related to "conversation."

t__lk　　di__log__e　　di__cus__ion

d__ba__e　　comm__nic__tion

Everyday Expressions

Read and memorize these expressions and sentences.

1. up to

   I think the president is *up to* no good again.

2. find out ...

   Check the Internet and *find out* who won today's game.

3. Remember ...

   Remember, always look both ways before you cross the street.

Mini-Application

Translate this sentence into English using the words and expressions above.

クラスに来るか来ないかはキミしだいだよ。だけど忘れないでね、出席は最終成績にはものすごく大事なんだよ。 （キミしだい＝ up to you、出席＝ attendance）

Verb Review

Do me a favor ...
お願いがあるんだけど…

自分ではとても無理なので、赤毛の女の子の気持ちをライナスに確かめてもらいたいチャーリー・ブラウン。Do me a favor は何かをお願いする時の決まり文句です。初めに Would you をつければもっと丁寧な言い方になります。do は疑問や否定文で使われる助動詞としての機能と“する”という動詞が基本ですが、特に口語では（will や should と共に用いて）通用する、役目を果たす（$20 will do it. 20 ドルで足りるよ）という意味でもよく使われます。

Listen and Repeat

Repeat these sentences after the audio. 32

1. Do your best.
2. Do as you like.
3. What do you think?
4. Do something about it now!
5. Do you know what I mean?
6. Don't worry. I will do the rest.

Listen and Write

Listen and fill in the blanks in these short dialogues. 33

1. M: Will five dollars be ( ) ( ) the tip?
   W: Yes, that will do just fine.
2. M: I heard you broke ( ) with David.
   W: I sure did. I don't want to have anything to do with him ( ).
3. W: Would you do me a big favor and give me a ( ) to the ( ) station?
   M: I'd be ( ) than happy to do it.
4. W: Do unto ( ) as you would ( ) them to do unto you.
   M: Isn't that a ( ) from the Bible? It sure sounds like it.

Cartoon 2

Read and enjoy this comic strip.

❶

* get a lot of valentines　ヴァレンタインデーに（チョコレートや花などの）沢山の贈り物をもらう
* that means ~　~という意味なのさ。
* solitary　一つの、唯一の

❷

❸

❹

いつもルーシーにやりこめられているので、ヤケになって喋っているチャーリー・ブラウン。そうだよ、今年のヴァレンタインデーだって何もなかったんだっ！そんなのわかってるわよ、と言わんばかりのルーシーは…

Reading

34

Good Grief! It's Valentine's Day!

楽しいはずのヴァレンタインデーだけど、チャーリー・ブラウンのポストの中はいつも空っぽ。でも来年こそは！ ロマンティックなイメージの強い日ですが、世界にはいろいろなヴァレンタインデーとそれにまつわる習慣がありそうです。

Valentine's Day comes every February, but not for Charlie Brown. He never receives any cards or chocolates. The sight of his empty mailbox makes him feel lonely and miserable. Of course, the little red-haired girl, whom he secretly adores, never sends him anything, either. Why would she? She doesn't even know he exists! Good grief! No wonder Charlie Brown hates this day!

Although Valentine's Day is associated with love and romance, its meaning and practices or customs vary from culture to culture. In North America, for example, couples such as husbands and wives or boyfriends and girlfriends exchange cards, chocolates, or flowers. But people in other social relationships—elementary-school classmates, friends, family members—also exchange such gifts as symbols of their bonds to one another. Almost immediately after New Year's, gift and stationery shops begin selling Valentine's Day cards that express these various human relationships. A card designed for a parent to give a child might read: *You're loved, and that's what Valentines are for.* Even after American children grow up and move far away from the parental home, they may still receive a card every year from Mom and Dad that reminds them of their parents' love.

In Finland, Valentine's Day only began to be marked on the calendar in 1987. There, it is called Friend's Day, a day largely free of romantic meaning. People reaffirm their ties of friendship by giving one another cards and small gifts. In Korea, meanwhile, there is a "holiday" called Black Day. What in the world is that? Well, on this day, April 14th, young Korean men and women who did not receive any chocolates on Valentine's Day get together at restaurants and eat noodles in black bean soup to cheer each other up. Black no doubt symbolizes sadness and disappointment. But as they enjoy their noodles, they give each other hope that next year they will find love on Valentine's Day.

It is too bad there is no Black Day in the world of *Peanuts*. It sounds like a day that is especially and perfectly suited to Charlie Brown's life and personality. Like young Koreans, he may not be so lucky in love again this year and feel sad and disappointed for it. But he also never gives up hope that next year his mailbox will be full of cards and chocolates—maybe even something from the little red-haired girl!

NOTES タイトル Good grief! なんてこと！ 3. adore 思い焦がれる、憧れる 10. bond 絆、結びつき 24. too bad 残念だ

Comprehension

Circle the best choice.

1. In North America, Valentine's Day _________.
   a. is celebrated only by people in romantic relationships
   b. can be for anyone you care about
   c. serves mainly for strengthening family ties

2. In Finland, Valentine's Day _________.
   a. emphasizes friendship
   b. isn't even marked on the calendar
   c. is supposed to be the most romantic day of the year

3. In South Korea, Black Day is _________.
   a. celebrated only by those who like black bean noodle soup
   b. the day you give chocolates to people you received a Valentine's card from
   c. a day for those who did not receive any chocolates on Valentine's Day

4. Which sentence best summarizes the main idea of the essay?
   a. Valentine's Day makes Charlie Brown feel left out.
   b. Valentine's Day cards aren't sold in North America until after New Year's.
   c. Valentine's Day is celebrated in a variety of ways throughout the world.

Think It Over

Q. What holiday do you especially like? What holiday don't you like? Why?

Q. Do you think Valentine's Day has become too commercialized that is, is it only an opportunity for card and candy makers and sellers to make a lot of money?

LESSON 12

Menu

- Keep sweeping me ...
- Woodstock, ultimate naturalist?

Cartoon 1

Read and enjoy this comic strip.

Setting the Scene

Hi, I am Pigpen. I have been here all the time, though my teacher has never even noticed my existence! Everyone hates dust and mud, but they are a big part of me. I live my life in a spirit of independence.

先生にボクの存在を気づいてもらえることもなかったけど、ボク、ピッグペンはずっと居たんだよ！ みんなが嫌がるホコリや泥はボクの一部で、独立心を持って生きてるつもりなんだ。

Guess the Words

Complete these words that are related to "notice."

aw_reness	ob_erv_tion	att_ntiv_ness
r_gard	c_nsciou_ness	abs_nt-minded

Everyday Expressions

Read and memorize these expressions and sentences.

❶ all year

I have been busy *all year*.

Strawberries are available *all year* in many places.

❷ sweep

My roommate cleans by *sweeping* dust and dirt under the carpet.

Mini-Application

Translate this sentence into English using the words and expressions above.

部屋を掃除している時、玄関のベルが鳴っているのに気がつかなかった。

Verb Review

The janitor **keeps** sweeping me out!
用務員さんにも‘掃除’され続けちゃった！

確かに体にはいっぱいホコリがついているけど、それが僕なんだ。誇り高く我が道を行く、ピッグペン登場です。ホコリだって僕の個性なんだけど、先生は僕のこと気づいてなかったみたいだし、学校のお掃除の時もいつも掃かれちゃう。ピッグペンのセリフの中の keep は、比較的長い期間何かを持ち続ける、保つ、ある動作をし続ける、というのが基本イメージです。保存・保管する、（ペットなどを）飼う、（家族などを）養う、ある場所や状態から離れない、という意味もあります。

Listen and Repeat

35

Repeat these sentences after the audio.

1. I kept on thinking about what she said.
2. Let's keep in touch through SNS!
3. Keep out! This is a private parking area.
4. Keep me posted on your progress.
5. I am keeping two of the puppies.
6. Thank you. Please keep the change.

Listen and Write

36

Listen and fill in the blanks in these short dialogues.

1. W: I sent my manuscript to a (   ), but it was rejected again.
   M: Sounds (   ). But keep on trying. You'll get some good news soon.

2. M: Make sure to keep up with your (   )! Next week we are going to talk about a new (   ).
   W: That's a lot of work, Professor Smith!

3. W: Hey, we've been (   ) for you. What kept you?
   M: Sorry. My internet (   ) was bad, so I wasn't able to get in for the (   ) of the meeting. So, what's on the table?

4. M: Please keep this (   ) to yourself for now. But I (   ) that Kelly is being transferred to the branch office in L.A.
   W: Good news. I know she has always liked the West Coast. I am really (   ) for her.

5. W: I like keeping a (   ) when I travel. I try to write down the (   ) of all the things that I experience.
M: That's a good habit. It's a wonderful way to keep (   ) close.

Cartoon 2

Read and enjoy this comic strip.

❶

❷

❸

❹

* on the other hand 一方では
* lead a full life 充実した人生を送る

オペラや映画は見たことないけど、
星や雨や虫のことなら知っている…
スヌーピーの友達、ウッドストック
は幸せそうです。

Reading

37

Woodstock, the Ultimate Naturalist?

真っすぐに飛ぶことは苦手だけど、いつか飛んでいってお母さんにも会ってみたい…黄色い渡り鳥ウッドストックの夢です。自然と繋がりながら生きるウッドストックは、私達が辛い時にもきっと何かのヒントを与えてくれそうです。

I'm sure you have noticed the little yellow bird in *Peanuts*. He appears quite frequently, and his name is Woodstock. Although he is supposed to be a migratory bird, one that flies south in the autumn and flies back up north in the spring, we seldom see Woodstock doing any actual migrating. One of his biggest dreams is to find his mother, whom he has never met. Woodstock has trouble flying in a straight line and, instead, flutters about like a butterfly. In the comic strips, his speech is represented by vertical marks rather than by letters and words, which makes it impossible for us to understand him. But Snoopy can, perfectly.

Woodstock isn't familiar with the pleasures and amusements that most of us enjoy. He has never been in a coffee shop or gone to a concert. He has, however, unlimited access to nature and can connect with all kinds of animals, from worms to cats and dogs. Being a part of and a participant in the natural world is Woodstock's primary source of joy.

Different cultures see nature in different ways. For example, in many Native American world views, human beings themselves are an integral part of nature. Thus, living harmoniously and in balance with nature is vital for keeping them healthy—body and soul.

The Ainu are an indigenous ethnic group in Hokkaido, Japan. They, too, have noteworthy ideas about nature and our place in it. In the Ainu language, "Ainu" simply means human. The Ainus believe that a sort of world spirit—*Kamuy* in their native language—not only lies in all natural phenomena like mountains and lakes but also in all animals, bears in particular. This is understandable. Bears provide the Ainu with food, clothing, tools, and other essentials and have always been at the center of the Ainus' most sacred ceremonies and rituals. Salmon are another precious friend of the Ainu. They wisely never catch more than they need, because to them, ensuring that nature's bounty never runs out is truly a matter of life and death.

As you can see, Native Americans and the Ainu alike have an ecologically sustainable way of living. They know how to live in harmony with the natural world. They may make use of the environment, but they do so in a way that doesn't damage or destroy or deplete it.

Woodstock can remind us that there is wisdom in the lives and values of people who embrace nature as a part of themselves and their communities. From the beginning, nature has connected the world. Today, we understand that the effects of improper stewardship—care—of the natural environment are not isolated to one country or region. The same goes for natural disasters. What affects one place has consequences for everyone on the planet. So, when we are hit by something frightening and unpredictable like the COVID-19 pandemic, let's remember Woodstock and Snoopy. We humans may have had to go without coffee shops and concerts for a while, but the sky, the stars, and all the other wonders of nature were and still are out there for us to enjoy, appreciate, and be a part of.

NOTES 5. flutter 羽ばたきする　15. noteworthy 注目に値する　17. Kamuy 精霊や神など霊的存在を意味するアイヌ語　32. pandemic 世界的（広域）流行病

Comprehension

Circle the best choice.

1. Which of these is NOT true about Woodstock?
   a. He migrates back and forth between north and south every year.
   b. He has a hard time flying in a straight line.
   c. He can make himself understood to Snoopy.

2. Which of the following concepts is NOT mentioned about Native Americans' world view?
   a. Their compatibility with nature and everything in it.
   b. Their dedication to hard work and being productive.
   c. Their ability to understand and get along with animals.

3. The Ainus are especially close to bears because
   a. Hokkaido's bears are not really wild animals.
   b. bears are the source of many of the things Ainus need to survive.
   c. Ainus train and use bears to fish for salmon for them.

4. Which sentence best summarizes the main idea of the essay?
   a. People could have a lot to learn from Woodstock and some indigenous peoples about how to practice a sustainable, environmentally friendly life.
   b. Going to coffee shops and concerts was not possible during the COVID-19 pandemic.
   c. Living in the countryside is best because it means that you will always be close and connected to nature.

Think It Over

Q. What other indigenous people can you think of in Japan and around the world?

Q. What ecologically friendly things do you practice?

COFFEE BREAK

Lucy's football trick ④
判断は難しい…

Making a decision is always difficult. Charlie Brown relies on his psychiatrist whenever he has a big decision to make, like, for example, whether he should try to kick the football. His confident "doctor" gives him a definite answer. Yes, she tells him, try. Armed with this advice, Charlie Brown is all "psyched up." This time ... But wait. Something's very wrong here.

armed with ~　～に力づけられて
"psyched up"　やる気充分になる、気合いを入れる
get me to kick ~　ボクに～を蹴らせようとする
land on my back　背中を地面に打ちつけてしまう、打撃をうける
sounds like ~　～みたい、～のような感じがする
get the impression　印象を受ける
medical terms　医学用語
clear to ~　～まで完全に

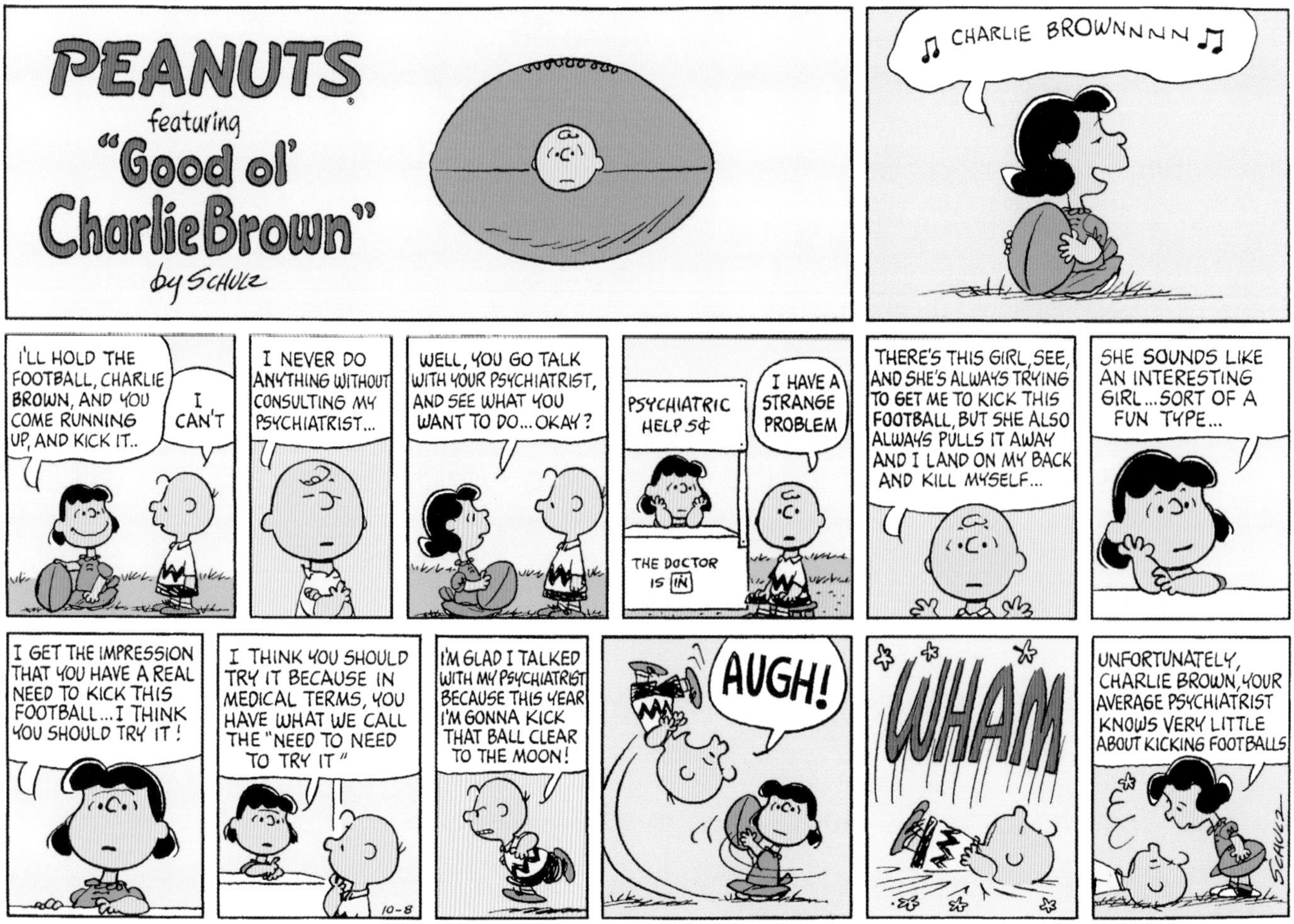

Search and Circle: Small Talk

Find the words in this "Search and Circle" puzzle that complete these sentences.

Sally hates ________________.

Schroeder loves ________________.

Lucy becomes a ________________ in her stand.

Snoopy pretends to be a ________________ and sometimes a flying ________________.

Linus has ________________ in the Great Pumpkin.

Charles Schulz has a great sense of ________________.

S	H	D	N	F	D
C	U	E	C	A	O
H	M	U	S	I	C
O	O	K	P	T	T
O	R	B	C	H	O
L	A	W	Y	E	R

LESSON 13

Menu

- Life goes on ...
- The Life and Work of Charles Schulz

Cartoon 1

Read and enjoy this comic strip.

Setting the Scene

Sally seems suddenly enlightened and philosophical. Now she knows that life continues no matter what happens, good or bad. Even when there's nothing good on TV!

サリーはいきなり教えを悟ったようです。そう、どんなことが起こっても人生は続くとわかったのです。楽しいことがあっても辛いことがあっても、たとえテレビで面白いのがやっていなくてもね！

Guess the Words

Complete these words that are related to "philosophy."

id__a　　th__ught　　no__ion　　vi__w

con__ept　　val__es　　pe__spe__tive

Everyday Expressions

Read and memorize these expressions and sentences.

❶ Good for you!

A: I had perfect attendance this year.
B: *Good for you!*

❷ What's on ...?

What's on at the mall theater this weekend?

❸ Nothing much.

A: So, what's up?
B: *Nothing much*. How about you?

Mini-Application

Sally's new philosophy is "Life goes on." Complete the following by making up a new philosophy of your own.

I have a new philosophy: "______________________________."

Verb Review

"Life **goes on**."
人生は続いてゆく

さあ、最後のレッスンです。何かを悟ったように見えるサリーですが、彼女はこれから学校や勉強が好きになってゆくでしょうか？ 彼女の最後のセリフ Life goes on. の go on は"続く"という意味ですね。go は"～に行く"というのが基本ですが、その後に形容詞が来ると（go well, go wrong など）"～という状態になる"という意味です。今回は go を使った決まり文句や表現を学びましょう。Here we go!

Listen and Repeat

Repeat these sentences after the audio.　38

1. Nice going!
2. What's going on?
3. Let's get going.
4. How's it going?
5. Go ahead.
6. I hope everything is going well for you.

Listen and Write

Listen and fill in the blanks in these short dialogues.　39

1. M: Before we go on, are there any (　　　　　　)?
   W: I (　　　　　　) one, Professor Smith.

2. W: How did your first (　　　　　　) go?
   M: Oh, it went very (　　　　　　).

3. W: Why did Mary get so (　　　　　　)?
   M: I'm (　　　　　　) my teasing went a little too far.

4. M: Did you go to your high school (　　　　　　) yesterday?
   W: No, I didn't. As time goes by, I (　　　　　　) more and more awkward about going.

Cartoon 2

Read and enjoy this comic strip.

* have me come down to　～に来させる
* no matter how ~　どんなに～でも
* be through ~　～（仕事など）を終える

お父さんの勤めている理髪店にやってきて彼の仕事が終わるまで待っているチャーリー・ブラウン。その姿は作者チャールズ・シュルツの少年時代のようです。

* worth　価値がある

一生懸命に働いて、欲しいものが全部手に入ったら人生の価値はあるの？チャーリー・ブラウンにはすぐには答えられません。あなたならどのように答えますか？ そしてスヌーピーの答えは…

Reading

40

The Life and Work of Charles Schulz

新聞での連載がなされて以来５０年間、ほとんど休みなどとることなしにピーナッツを描き続けた“スパーキー”こと漫画家チャールズ・シュルツ。チャーリー・ブラウンと沢山の共通点を持つ彼が創りあげた愛すべきピーナッツの世界、そして彼の生涯とは？

Even if before you took this class you had never read a single *Peanuts* strip,—though that sounds unimaginable!—you were surely familiar with the black-and-white beagle and his round-headed boy “master.” Charles Schulz first created these immortal characters decades ago. He learned to draw comics through a correspondence course after graduating from high school. His father, a barber just like Charlie Brown’s dad, worked hard to help pay his son’s tuition and encouraged young Schulz to practice conscientiously and cultivate his talent.

After many rejections, Schulz’s *Li’l Folks*, a strip that was the predecessor of *Peanuts*, finally ran in his hometown paper, the *St. Paul Pioneer Press*, from 1947 to 1949. On October 2, 1950, *Peanuts* premiered in seven newspapers across the United States. At its peak, *Peanuts* ran in over 2,600 daily newspapers, attracting more than 335 million readers in 75 countries. It was translated into 40 languages, and today reprints of the strip still run in newspapers all over the world. Without the help of any assistant or hardly ever taking days off, Schulz drew tirelessly and happily for fifty years. During this time *Peanuts* became part of the cultural landscape of the U.S. Snoopy “went to the moon” and Linus’s “security blanket” became part of the American vernacular.

While many cartoonists stress adventure, slapstick, or detailed scenery, Schulz focused on telling the truth about life in subtle ways. One of his consistent themes is disappointment. Charlie Brown’s baseball team always loses. Peppermint Patty’s tests always receive D minuses. All the love in the strip — Lucy’s for Schroeder, Sally’s for Linus, and Charlie Brown’s for the little red-haired girl — is unrequited. The Great Pumpkin never appears. The football is always pulled away at the last moment. Yet no matter how disappointing the situations are, Charlie Brown and his friends never give up. Charlie Brown still hopes his baseball team will win, still dreams of talking one day to the little red-haired girl, and is still determined to kick that football. He keeps his hopes up because he is not a loser. A loser, in Schulz’s way of thinking, is not the person who fails, but a person who stops trying.

Although Schulz passed away on February 12, 2000, his message lives on. “To take a blank piece of paper and draw characters that people love and worry about is extremely satisfying. It really does not matter what you are called, or where your work is placed, as long as it brings some kind of joy to some person some place.” In his farewell cartoon strip he acknowledged the joy the *Peanuts*’ characters had brought him. “... Charlie Brown, Snoopy, Linus, Lucy ... how can I ever forget them ...” Indeed, how could we ever forget them—or the man who created them?

NOTES 6. tuition 授業料　7. predecessor 前身　14. Snoopy “went to the moon” 1969 年のアポロ 10 号の打ち上げで、指令船がチャーリー・ブラウン、月面探査機がスヌーピーと名付けられ宇宙空間で彼らの名前が呼び交わされた。
15. vernacular 言葉、日常語　20. unrequited 報われない、見返りのない

Comprehension

Circle the best choice.

1. Like Charlie Brown’s dad, Charles Schulz’s father worked __________.
   a. as a cartoonist
   b. as the principal of a high school
   c. as a barber

2. Which of the following statements is true?
   a. Charles Schulz worked every day.
   b. Charles Schulz hired assistants every now and then.
   c. Charles Schulz never experienced any rejections.

3. Which of these best describes *Peanuts*?
   a. adventurous and thrilling
   b. subtle and suggestive
   c. dramatic and sincere

4. Which sentence best summarizes the main idea of the essay?
   a. *Peanuts* describes an ideal world that can work as a model for all of us to aspire to.
   b. Without his father’s help and encouragement, Charles Schulz would never have become a cartoonist, let alone a successful one.
   c. Charles Schulz consistently believed that though life is full of disappointment, which he subtly portrayed through his characters, we should never give up trying.

Think It Over

Q. Have you ever experienced an “unrequited” relationship of any kind? Explain.

Q. Which *Peanuts* character(s) do you most identify with? Why?

NOTE

NOTE

NOTE

The following titles were helpful in framing my essays around cultural themes.

References

Books

Apte, Mahadev. *Humor and Laughter: An Anthropological Approach.* Ithaca, NY: Cornell University Press, 1985.

Blount, Ben. *Language, Culture, and Society. A Book of Readings.* Long Grove, IL: Waveland Press, Inc., 1995.

Barfield, Thomas, ed. *The Dictionary of Anthropology.* Malden, MA: Blackwell Publishers, 1997.

Chung, Leeva and Stella Ting-Toomey. *Understanding Intercultural Communication.* Los Angeles, CA: Roxbury Publishing Company, 2005.

Damen, Louise. *Culture Learning: The Fifth Dimension in the Language Classroom.* Reading, MA: Addison-Wesley Publishing Company, 1987.

Gudykunst, William. *Bridging Differences: Effective Intergroup Communication.* Thousand Oaks, CA: Sage Publications, 2004.

Hinkel, Eli. *Culture in Second Language Teaching and Learning.* New York: Cambridge University Press, 2003.

Inge, Thomas. *Charles M. Schulz Conversations.* Jackson: University Press of Mississippi, 2000.

Johnson, Rheta. *Good Grief: The Story of Charles M. Schulz.* Missouri: Andrews and McMeel A Universal Syndicate Company, 1989.

Kottak, Conrad. *Anthropology: The Exploration of Human Diversity.* New York: Random House, Inc., 2006.

Kluckhohn, Clyde. *Mirror for Man: The Relation of Anthropology to Modern Life.* New York: McGraw-Hill Book Company, 1949.

Lincoln, Kenneth. *Indi'n Humor: Bicultural Play in Native America.* New York: Oxford University Press, 1993.

Millar, Barbara. *Cultural Anthropology.* New York: Pearson Education, 2005.

Schulz, Charles. *Peanuts: A Golden Celebration. The Art and the Story of the World's Best-Loved Comic Strip.* New York: HarperCollins Publishers, Inc., 1999.

Schulz, Charles. *You Really Don't Look 50, Charlie Brown.* West Sussex: Ravette Publishing Limited, 2000.

Schulz, Charles. *Peanuts: Anniversary Treasury.* West Sussex: Ravette Publishing Limited, 2001.

Schulz, Charles. *Peanuts: The Art of Charles M. Schulz, with an Introduction by Jean Schulz.* New York: Panthcon Books, 2003.

Schulz, Charles. *Happiness is a Warm Puppy.* Maine: Cider Mill Press Book Publishers, 2006.

Schulz, Charles. *My life with Charlie Brown.* (edited and with an introduction by M.Thomas Inge). Jackson: University Press of Mississippi, 2010.

Short, Robert. *The Gospel According to Peanuts.* Louisville, Kentucky: Westminster John Knox Press, 1965.

The Holy Bible (King James Version). 3rd Edition. Philadelphia: Westminster Press, 1948.

Wainwright, Gordon. *Body Language.* NTC/Contemporary Publishing, 1993.

Sites regarding *Peanuts* and Charles Schulz

www.snoopy.com
www.schulzmuseum.org

LESSON 1 Cartoon 1: year=1995.2.9, Cartoon 2: year=1964.2.1

LESSON 2 Cartoon 1: year=1968.2.7, Cartoon 2: year=1969.2.11

LESSON 3 Cartoon 1: year=1968.11.27, Cartoon 2: year=1989.4.15,

COFFEE BREAK year=1977.10.09

LESSON 4 Cartoon 1: year=1968.8.15, Cartoon 2: year=1995.12.11

LESSON 5 Cartoon 1: year=1995.6.9, Cartoon 2: year=1974.4.17

LESSON 6 Cartoon 1: year=1995.2.7, Cartoon 2: year=1969.9.17

COFFEE BREAK year=1980.11.16

LESSON 7 Cartoon 1: year=1995.1.19, Cartoon 2: year=1985.2.18

LESSON 8 Cartoon 1: year=1968.10.2, Cartoon 2: year=1964.4.14

LESSON 9 Cartoon 1: year=1995.5.8, Cartoon 2: year=1968.9.3

COFFEE BREAK year=1989.10.1

LESSON 10 Cartoon 1: year=1967.8.23, Cartoon 2: year=1963.10.31

LESSON 11 Cartoon 1: year=1963.12.4, Cartoon 2: year=1964.2.15

LESSON 12 Cartoon 1: year=1984.11.15, Cartoon 2: year=1972.8.15

COFFEE BREAK year=1972.10.8

LESSON 13 Cartoon 1: year=1996.8.2, Cartoon 2: year=1968.1.27, year=1995.12.13

Enjoy English with Charlie Brown and Friends
— Language and Culture in *Peanuts* <Revised Edition>
『ピーナッツ』で学ぶ英語と比較文化〔改訂新版〕 [B-932]

1 刷 2022年2月17日
2 刷 2023年3月13日

著 者 外山 晴子 Haruko Toyama

発行者 南雲 一範 Kazunori Nagumo
発行所 株式会社 南雲堂
〒162-0801 東京都新宿区山吹町361
NAN'UN-DO Co., Ltd.
361 Yamabuki-cho, Shinjuku-ku, Tokyo 162-0801, Japan
振替口座：00160-0-46863
TEL: 03-3268-2311（営業部：学校関係）
03-3268-2384（営業部：書店関係）
03-3268-2387（編集部）
FAX: 03-3269-2486
編集者 加藤 敦

組 版 スタジオAina, スタジオA.Kato

装 丁 銀 月 堂

検 印 省 略

コード ISBN978-4-523-17932-0 C0082

Printed in Japan

E-mail : nanundo@post.email.ne.jp
URL : https://www.nanun-do.co.jp/